A Theatre503 production

T0352666

OUT OF SORTS

BY DANUSIA SAMAL

Out of Sorts was the winner of the Theatre503 International
Playwriting Award 2018 and was first performed at Theatre503,
London, on 9 October 2019.

OUT OF SORTS

BY DANUSIA SAMAL

CAST

ZARA	Nalân Burgess
LAYLA	Myriam Acharki
HUSSEIN	Nayef Rashed
FATIMA	Oznur Cifci
ALICE	Emma Denly
ANTHONY	Claudius Peters

CREATIVE TEAM

Director	Tanuja Amarasuriya
Designer	Rebecca Wood
Lighting Designer	Ali Hunter
Sound Designer	Rachael Murray
Casting Director	Lilly Mackie
Fight Director	Enric Ortuño

PRODUCTION TEAM

Producer	Jake Orr
Production Manager	Callum Finn
Stage Manager	Keira Dulake
PR	Nancy Poole
Assistant Producer	Frankie Greig

This production has been made possible with the support of The Foyle Foundation, Arts Council England National Lottery Project Grant, Garrick Charitable Trust, Cockayne Grants for the Arts and the London Community Foundation.

CAST

NALÂN BURGESS – ZARA

Stage credits include: Where We Are (The Mosque at the Arcola); My Beautiful Laundrette (Above The Stag); Citizen (The Space).

Short play credits include: Who's Mom and Who's Mama (Theatre503); Aleema The Boy Girl (Brave New World) and Sexual Assault (The Pleasance).

Musical credits include: Nine, Sweet Charity and South Pacific (Edinburgh Festival Fringe).

Television credits include: Rude Boys (BBC Three).

Festival credits include: Taarof (BFI Nights, Underwire).

Voiceover credits include the cult video game Elite: Dangerous and The Offensive (British Podcast Awards' 2019 winner).

MYRIAM ACHARKI – LAYLA

Myriam was born in Brussels where she trained first in Artistic Humanities then at L'Insas for a year, before moving to London to study with Philippe Gaulier (Lecoq school).

Stage credits include: Returning to Haifa (Finborough); KABEIROI (Punchdrunk); Dionysos Unbound (Bridewell); Woyzeck (Drama Desk Awards Nominee, St Ann's, New York); Jane Eyre (Shared Experience); Woyczek (The Gate); The Seven Year Itch (West End); Macbeth False Memory (ATC); Princess Sharon (Scarlet); Peter Pan (West Yorkshire Playhouse); The Decameron (The Gate); and The House of Bernarda Alba (Aspect).

Television credits include: Sex Education (Netflix); Next of Kin (ITV); Chasing Shadows (ITV); Silk (BBC Drama); Sinbad (Sky/BBC); New Tricks (Wall to Wall/BBC); E20, Doctors, Paradise Heights, Holby City, Attachment (BBC); Under Suspicion (LaPlante Productions); Little Miss Jocelyn (Brown Eyed Boy Productions); Human Cargo (Gemini Awards Nominee, C.B.C/Alliance Films); Northsquare (Channel 4); Sex and Chocolate and This Could be The Last Time (BBC Screen One).

Film credits include: John Carter of Mars (Pixar/Disney); The Beach (Figment Films); City of Tiny Lights (Sixteen Films) and 28 k (Formosa Film).

NAYEF RASHED – HUSSEIN

Nayef trained at the Drama Centre London.

Television credits include: The Looming Tower and Stella.

Film credits include: The Story of My Wife; Waiting for the Barbarians; Salmon Fishing in the Yemen and The Parole Officer.

Nayef is currently setting up a drama club for children that can't afford drama school fees.

OZNUR CIFCI – FATIMA

Oznur trained under the Lee Strasberg Method at the Brian Timoney Actors' Studio. She speaks fluent English and Turkish and has professional credits in both English and Turkish productions.

Film credits include the Turkish feature film Iki Nefes Arasinda.

Screen credits include: Tattoo Fixers and Real Dealz.

Upcoming credits include: writing and producing her own short film A Monstrous Mind and the lead role in the feature film Crushed Wings.

EMMA DENLY – ALICE

Emma trained at RADA where she was a Leverhulme and Wall Trust scholar.

Stage credits include: The Rebellious Women of Wimbledon (Offie Nominee, Attic); The Rivals (Watermill); The Woman in the Moon (Shakespeare's Globe); Saint George and the Dragon (workshop at National Theatre Studio); The Importance of Being Earnest (Theatr Clwyd); Women Redressed (Park); A Christmas Carol (Reading Arts) and Read Not Dead (readings at Shakespeare's Globe).

Screen credits include: UK: A-Z-Pilot and Christmas Hacks (Baldy Productions, YouTube); Golden Girl London Film School.

Emma also writes for theatre and television, and works as a voiceover artist.

CLAUDIUS PETERS – ANTHONY

Claudius is an actor based in London.

Stage credits include: Little Baby Jesus (Birmingham Repertory Theatre) and Drip Drip Drip (national tour, Pipeline).

Film credits include: Fantastic Beasts: Crimes of Grindelwald; Dying of the Light; Stay Woke and The Touch (The Berlin Film Festival).

CREATIVE TEAM

DANUSIA SAMAL – WRITER

Danusia Samal is an actress, writer and singer who has performed at the Royal Court, Royal Shakespeare Company, Globe, and Soho Theatre.

Screen credits include: The Great (Hulu); Ghost in the Shell (Paramount/DreamWorks) and Tyrant (FOX).

In 2018, Danusia wrote and performed Busking It, a gig theatre piece inspired by her experiences as a London Underground busker. Busking It was commissioned by Shoreditch Town Hall and co-produced by HighTide, with critical acclaim in Edinburgh and London. Danusia went on to win the Theatre503 International Playwriting Award for Out of Sorts and was later selected by the BBC for their 2019 TV Drama Writers' Programme, receiving a commission to write a TV series inspired by the play. Danusia is an alumnus of BBC London Voices, Tamasha Playwrights and Soho Writers' Lab.

Other writing credits include: The Museum (Tamasha Theatre/SOAS University); Conditionally (Soho/Oxford School of Drama) and Langthorne Stories (Soho/Waltham Forest).

TANUJA AMARASURIYA – DIRECTOR

Tanuja is a Director and Sound Designer who works across theatre, film and digital sound. As a Director and Dramaturg she has worked with playwrights and theatremakers including Improbable, Timothy X Atack, Dipika Guha, Sam Halmarack, Eno Mfon, Marietta Kirkbride and Raucous. As Sound Designer, her credits include work with Selina Thompson, Inua Ellams/Fuel and Chris Thorpe & Rachel Chavkin. She is co-Artistic Director of Sleepdogs, a wide-ranging collaboration with writer and composer Timothy X Atack, making theatre, film and audio work characterised by imaginative storytelling and visceral, emotional, sensory aesthetics. Sleepdogs' work has been developed and presented nationally and internationally, including at the National Theatre (London), Bristol Old Vic, Seattle International Film Festival, Royal Exchange Theatre, Manchester, Channel 4 television, BBC Radio, NexT International Film Festival (Bucharest), BIOS (Athens) and Sura Medura (Sri Lanka). She is a Leverhulme Arts Scholar attached to Bristol Old Vic and a resident at Watershed's Pervasive Media Studio.

RACHAEL MURRAY – SOUND DESIGNER

Rachael Murray is a Sound Artist and Designer, currently based in Glasgow. She trained at the Royal Academy of Dramatic Art.

Sound design credits include: Bible John (Poor Michelle, Edinburgh Festival Fringe); Resurrecting Bobby Awl (Avalon, BBC Arts and Edinburgh Festival Fringe); A Lesson from Aloes and Jeannie (Finborough); Drowned or Saved? (Tristan Bates); Quietly, The Yellow Wallpaper and The Soul of Wittgenstein (Clapham Omnibus); Immaculate Correction, and Mermaids (The King's Head); Woman Before a Glass (Jermyn Street) and House of America (Brockley Jack).

ALI HUNTER – LIGHTING DESIGNER

Ali's lighting design credits include: For Services Rendered, The Play About My Dad and Woman Before a Glass (Jermyn Street); Cash Cow (Hampstead); Muckers (The Egg, Conde Duque and Oxford Playhouse); Soft Animals (Soho); Don't Forget the Birds and Rattlesnake (Open Clasp); I know not these my hands, Happy Fathers' Day, Sugarman and All in Minor (The Place); Clear White Light (Live Theatre, Newcastle); Treemonisha and The Boatswain's Mate (Arcola); Isaac Came Home from the Mountain and Cinderella and the Beanstalk (Theatre503); Gracie and The Biograph Girl (Finborough); Tenderly (New Wimbledon Studio); Katzenmusik (Royal Court) and Foreign Body (Southbank Centre for WOW).

Credits as Associate Lighting Designer includes: Hot Mess for Candoco Dance and The Half God of Rainfall (Birmingham Rep and Kiln).

Ali is the Young Associate Lighting Designer for Matthew Bourne's Romeo and Juliet.

LILLY MACKIE – CASTING DIRECTOR

Lilly started as Casting Assistant at Annelie Powell Casting in 2019 after four years as an Agent's Assistant. Since joining Annelie, her Casting Assistant credits include: The Weatherman (Park); One Man Two Guvnors (New Wolsey and Nuffield Southampton Theatres); Pavilion (Theatr Clwyd); Cinderella (Nuffield Southampton Theatres) and Vassa (Almeida).

Her film credits include Dragonkeeper (Gkids) and Deep Blue Sea 3 (Warner Bros).

This is her Theatre503 debut as Casting Director.

ENRIC ORTUÑO – FIGHT DIRECTOR

Enric Ortuño is a Fight and Intimacy Director and certified Stage Combat Teacher by the British Academy of Stage and Screen Combat. He holds a four-year BA in Musical Theatre from the Spanish Conservatoire of Dramatic Art and a MA in Movement Studies by the Royal Central School of Speech and Drama. He teaches at Drama Studio London and Italia Conti and has taught workshops in Spain, Canada, USA and Germany.

Recent credits include: The Weatherman (Park); The Amber Trap (Theatre503); Jane Eyre (Blackeyed); Jekyll & Hyde, Dracula (Arrows & Traps); The Drag (Arcola); Boris: World King (Trafalgar Studios); Croydon Avengers (Ovalhouse); Treasure Island (Oxford Theatre Guild); Love me Now (Tristan Bates); Dangerous Giant Animals (Underbelly, Edinburgh); Titus Andronicus, Othello (Smooth Faced Gentlemen); Monster (Worklight); Verdi's Macbeth (Iford Arts); The Autumn Garden (Jermyn Street) and Escape the Scaffold (Theatre503).

PRODUCTION TEAM

JAKE ORR – PRODUCER

Jake is Producer for Theatre503 and Jake Orr Productions. He will shortly be joining Nottingham Playhouse as their first Producer. Before joining Theatre503 Jake was a freelance producer and programmer. In 2009 Jake founded A Younger Theatre and in 2014 he co-founded Incoming Festival with New Diorama Theatre.

Jake's producing credits include: Pops (Edinburgh Festival Fringe and HighTide Festival, winner: The Stage Edinburgh Award); Wolfie, Cinderella and the Beanstalk (Theatre503); Br'er Cotton (Theatre503, winner: Best New Play Off West End Awards); In Event of Moone Disaster (Theatre503, winner: Best New Writer The Stage Debut Awards); No Miracles Here (The Letter Room at Edinburgh Festival Fringe, Northern Stage, The Lowry and Shoreditch Town Hall); BLUSH (Snuff Box Theatre at Edinburgh Fringe Festival, Soho and on tour; winner: The Stage Award for Best Performance); Weald (Snuff Box and Finborough) and Shelter Me (Circumference and Theatre Delicatessen). He has also produced Dialogue Festival (Ovalhouse).

As co-producer his credits include J'Ouvert, The Art of Gaman (Theatre503); Gutted (HOME, Manchester and Edinburgh Festival Fringe); COW (Edinburgh Festival Fringe) and Sticking (national tour).

As Associate Producer his credits include Lists for the End of the World (Edinburgh Festival Fringe); The Bombing of the Grand Hotel (Cockpit Theatre and tour); Mouse Plague (Edinburgh Festival Fringe, BAC and tour) and The Eradication of Schizophrenia in Western Lapland (Edinburgh Festival Fringe, BAC and tour).

Jake was nominated for Best Producer in the 2014 Off West End Awards.

CALLUM FINN – PRODUCTION MANAGER

Callum is a Freelance Production Manager.

Current Projects include: Prime Pantomimes 2019 Season; Madagascar the Musical (international tour); Toast (UK tour); The Storm Whale (York Theatre Royal) and Beauty and the Beast (Oxford Playhouse).

Recent theatre credits include: Alice in Wonderland, A Midsummer Night's Dream and Pinocchio (Immersion Theatre UK tour); Bare: A Pop Opera (The Vaults); Peace at Last (Opera Up Close UK tour); Tumulus (Soho); Virtual Conservatoire (Royal College of Music); Wolfie (Theatre503); All in a Row (Southwark Playhouse); Grandad's Island (Engine House Theatre, UK and Geneva tour); A Crag Path Christmas (AJH); Cinderella and the Beanstalk (Theatre503); Seussical (Southwark Playhouse); Euroboat (Viking Line Cruises); Daisy Pulls It Off (Park) and Hamlet (KBTC).

Film credits include: Artemis Fowl (Disney) and All is True (TKBC).

Previously Callum worked as Assistant Head of Production at RADA. He also holds a BA (Hons) in Production and Stage Management from the Royal Academy of Dramatic Art.

KEIRA DULAKE – STAGE MANAGER

Keira is a Stage Manager from Surrey who has recently graduated from the Guildford School of Acting.

Her credits as a trainee Stage Manager include: Shrek the Musical and a work placement on The Return of Ulysses (Royal Opera House).

She currently works on a variety of productions from Fringe to Opera and enjoys the diversity that live theatre has to offer.

Further Stage Manager credits include: Silk Road (New Generation Festival, Florence).

Assistant Stage Manager credits include: Le Nozze di Figaro (New Generation Festival, Florence).

Keira is delighted to be joining the team at Theatre503 as Stage Manager for Out of Sorts.

FRANKIE GREIG – ASSISTANT PRODUCER

Frankie is one of the current Resident Assistant Producers at Theatre503. Having recently graduated from Newcastle University with a degree in Biomedical Sciences, she also spent three years as a member of Newcastle University Theatre Society. There she worked as an Assistant Producer and Producer on an array of shows, including Hairspray: The Musical and the Ealing comedy classic The Ladykillers at venues such as The Cluny and Newcastle College Theatre. She has also regularly worked with new student writing across drama festivals and Edinburgh Fringe previews, which makes working at Theatre503 all the more exciting. This is Frankie's first role within a professional theatre, and she can't wait to continue producing as part of such a fantastic team.

THEATRE 503

Theatre503 is the home of new writers and a launchpad for the artists who bring their words to life. We are pioneers in supporting new writers and a champion of their role in the theatre ecology. We find exceptional playwrights who will define the canon for the next generation. Learning and career development are at the core of what we do. We stage the work of more debut and emerging writers than any other theatre in the country. In the last year alone we staged over 60 productions featuring 133 writers from short plays to full runs of superb drama and launching over 1,000 artists in the process. We passionately believe the most important element in a writer's development is to see their work developed through to a full production on stage, performed to the highest professional standard in front of an audience.

Over the last decade many first-time writers have gone on to establish a career in the industry thanks to the support of Theatre503: Tom Morton-Smith (**Oppenheimer**, RSC & West End), Anna Jordan (Bruntwood Prize Winner for **Yen**, Royal Exchange, Royal Court and Broadway), Vinay Patel (writer of the BAFTA winning **Murdered By My Father**), Katori Hall (**Mountaintop**, 503, West End & Broadway – winner of 503's first Olivier Award) and Jon Brittain (**Rotterdam** – winner of our second Olivier Award in 2017).

THEATRE503 TEAM

Artistic Director	Lisa Spirling
Executive Director	Andrew Shepherd
Producer	Jake Orr
Literary Manager	Steve Harper
Carne Associate Director	Anastasia Osei-Kuffour
General Manager	Molly Jones
Marketing Coordinator	Jennifer Oliver
Technical Manager	Alex Farrell
Literary Associate	Lauretta Barrow
Box Office Supervisor	Daisy Milner
Resident Assistant Producers	Frankie Greig and Beth Cooper

THEATRE503 BOARD

Erica Whyman OBE (Chair)
Royce Bell (Vice Chair)
Chris Campbell
Joachim Fleury
Celine Gagnon
Eleanor Lloyd
Marcus Markou
Geraldine Sharpe-Newton
Jack Tilbury
Roy Williams OBE

THEATRE503 VOLUNTEERS

Hannah Bates, Suzie Brewis, Georgia Cusworth, Debra Dempster, Rachel Gemaehling, Gareth Jones, Tom Lynam, Graham McCulloch, Tom Mellors, Annabel Pemberton, Meli Pinkerton, Hannah Randall, Gaye Russell, Hannah Sands, Caroline Summers, Thanos Topouzis, Melisa Tehrani, Camilla Walters.

OUR SUPPORTERS

We are incredibly grateful to the following who have supported us recently without whom our work would not have been possible.

We are particularly grateful to Philip and Christine Carne and the long term support of The Carne Trust for our Playwriting Award, the 503 Five and Carne Associate.

Share The Drama Patrons: Angela Hyde-Courtney, Eilene Davidson, Cas & Philip Donald, Erica Whyman, Geraldine Sharpe-Newton, Jack Tilbury/Plann, Jennifer Jacobs, Jill Segal, Joachim Fleury, Jon and NoraLee Sedmak, Liberty Oberlander, Marcus Markou & Dynamis, Marianne Badrichani, Mike Morfey, Pam Alexander & Roger Booker, Patricia Hamzahee, Richard Bean, Robert O'Dowd, The Bell Family, Sean Winnett and all our 503 Friends and Share The Drama supporters.

The Foyle Foundation, Arts Council England Grants for the Arts, Garrick Charitable Trust, Cockayne Grants for the Arts (503 Productions), Noël Coward Foundation (Rapid Write Response) The Orseis Trust (503Five), Battersea Power Station Foundation (Right to Write), Wimbledon Foundation (Five-O-Fresh), Nick Hern Books (503 Playwriting Award), Wandsworth Borough Council, The Theatres Trust.

THEATRE503 INTERNATIONAL PLAYWRITING AWARD

Five extraordinary new voices made up the finalists of Theatre503's 2018 International Playwriting Award supported by The Carne Trust and Nick Hern Books. Mathilde Dratwa, Gillian Greer, Joel MacCormack, Philana Imade Omorotionmwan and Danusia Samal were been chosen from 2,055 scripts sent in from 49 countries. Danusia Samal was announced as the winner on November 22nd at The Bridge Theatre, selected by a panel chaired by Erica Whyman (Chair of Theatre503 and Deputy Artistic Director, RSC). The panel were Lyn Gardner, Stephen Beresford, Abigail Gonda, Chinonyerem Odimba, Roy Williams, Alice Birch and Lisa Spirling. Danusia followed 2014's joint winners Paul Murphy (Valhalla) and Bea Roberts (And Then Come The Nightjars) and 2016 winner Andrew Thompson (In Event of Moone Disaster, winner of Best Writer at The 2018 Stage Debut Awards).

The readers for the Theatre503 International Playwriting Award included: Joel Ormsby; Rebecca Latham; Martin Edwards; Monique Sterling; Rikki Henry; Kate Budgen; Jenny Davis; Uju Enendu; Nika Obydzinski; Tommo Fowler; Tom Latter; Rosie Wyatt; Yasmeen Arden; Naomi Sumner; Paula B Stanic; Erick Kwashie; Neil Grutchfield; John Jack Paterson; Lisa Cagnacci; Joshua Higgott; Audrey Thayer and Lauretta Barrow.

Theatre503 would like to thank Chinonyerem Odimba, Ashna Rabheru, Bethany Cullinane, Hayat Kamille, Souad Faress and Theo Ogundipe for their support and work during the rehearsed reading of the play. Further thanks to Sarah Dickenson; Sita Calvert-Ennals and Tim X Atack.

OUT OF SORTS

Danusia Samal

Thanks and Acknowledgements

This play has been in my head for a long, long time and there were a lot of people who helped bring it here! People who read terrible early drafts, who offered their notes, feedback and support, who listened to me moan about how it wasn't working! So, in no particular order, special thanks to: The whole team at 503 who were so welcoming and supportive, especially Lisa, Steve, Jake, Andrew and Jennifer; the judges who picked *Out of Sorts* as 503's winning play and gave me the shock of my life; to Nic Wass and Jane Fallowfield who read early drafts – your feedback was invaluable; Fin Kennedy at Tamasha; Nick Hern Books; Chino Odimba; Alex Rusher; all the mates who read and performed sections (Josh, Sarah I'm looking at you!); Tanuja and all the brilliant cast and creative team who have brought the text to life and dealt with lots and lots of hummus-y mess; and last but not least my family, who have taught me to be 'out of sorts' and proud.

Danusia

Characters

ZARA, *mid/late twenties*
LAYLA, *Zara's mother. Fifties*
HUSSEIN, *Zara's father. Fifties*
FATIMA, *Zara's little sister. Seventeen*
ALICE, *Zara's best friend and flatmate. Mid/late twenties*
ANTHONY, *Alice's boyfriend. Thirties*

Note on Play

The family's country of origin is intentionally unspecified.
The company is free to make a decision about which Arabic-speaking country Zara's family is from, and to adjust any cultural references accordingly.

Forward slashes (/) indicate the point at which the next speaker interrupts.

Words in [square brackets] are unspoken.

Some Arabic words or phrases are used in the text. The company is free to change these, or to translate other sections of the text from English to Arabic.

Text in ***bold italics*** indicates characters are speaking in Arabic.

Set

The stage is split, simultaneously representing two rooms in two very different households. We see the living room of Zara's family home. A small, slightly worn council flat, but very very clean and tidy. Bits of kitsch furniture: doilies, a golden-framed picture of Mecca, a large dining table. One door leads to the kitchen, the other to the front entrance.

Coexisting onstage is Zara's British home. A small kitchen in a flat she shares with her best friend Alice. By contrast it is very IKEA and millennial. Messy. Girls' clothes, papers strewn everywhere. There's a breakfast bar and stools, bits of furniture the girls have put there ad hoc. The result is a space they own, occupy, and relax in.

This text went to press before the end of rehearsals and so may differ slightly from the play as performed.

ACT ONE

1. Saturday morning

Lights up and ALICE *enters, wearing running clothes and nibbling a jam doughnut. She heads to the counter to prepare a sandwich.* ZARA's *phone is on the counter.*

Meanwhile, in another part of the space, FATIMA *enters carrying an iPad, headphones in her ears. She is preoccupied, working something through. Checking nobody is coming, she takes a seat at the dining table and talks to herself, in time with the beat she is listening to:*

FATIMA. You ask me where I'm from... where do I begin? Skin...? Sin? Shin... shit.

FATIMA kisses her teeth and writes on her iPad. Meanwhile, ZARA's *phone begins to buzz.* ALICE *clocks it. The buzzing annoys her. It stops.*

ZARA *enters. For a moment she stands between the two worlds, unsure of herself.* FATIMA *freezes, as if hearing a noise offstage. A moment of stillness. Then:*

ALICE. Morning, lovely!

ZARA *moves over to* ALICE *and slumps across the kitchen counter.* FATIMA *continues mouthing the lyrics she is writing, quietly.* ALICE *quickly moves so* ZARA *cannot see the doughnut in her hand.*

ZARA. Urgh.

ALICE. That bad eh?

ZARA (*face down on the counter*). I feel like shit!

ALICE. Is that guilt? Or a raging hangover?

ZARA. I don't get hangovers.

ALICE. Well, they do say, once you reach a certain *age*...

ZARA. Shut it.

ALICE. Charmer! There, that's for you.

ZARA. Wassat?

ALICE. Smashed avocado on sourdough. A 'well done, Zara!' breakfast!

ZARA hesitates for a beat, before smiling broadly and grabbing the plate.

ZARA. You are literally an angel. What about you?

ALICE. Not really hungry. Had a bit of muesli after my run this morning – what?

ZARA. You smug bitch! As if I can eat it now!

ALICE. You're skinny as anything!

ZARA. Have you seen me lately?! I'm putting away carbs like –

ALICE. Shut up and eat the fucking avo.

ZARA takes a big bite. ALICE watches in envy.

How do you do it? I've had nothing but rabbit food for three weeks and I've put on half a stone!

ZARA shows her hands to ALICE, which are covered in avocado.

Kitchen roll's there.

ZARA grabs a large bit of kitchen roll, wipes her mouth and throws it in the bin. Her phone buzzes again.

Ugh! Please make it stop! It's been going all morning!

Without even looking at the phone, ZARA cancels the call. ALICE clocks this, leans in for gossip.

Is it him? Is it Jamil calling you?

ZARA (*evasive*). Dunno.

ALICE. So how was it? Did he cry?

ZARA. No.

ALICE. Should've. He's not gonna find anyone better than you, ever... What? I know it sounds mean but it's true! Jamil's not for you, babe, no matter how much your family want it. You did the right thing. (*Finding this very funny.*) Can you imagine if you'd actually seen it through? The huge tacky wedding, becoming *Mrs Estate Agent*, moving to Brent with Jamil and his mum?! (*At* ZARA*'s face.*) Hey, I'm sorry, I actually am. I know, you feel bad for hurting him, and yes, your family *will* think you're haram for a little bit –

ZARA (*laughing*). I wish I'd never taught you that word!

ALICE *sings the word 'Haram' like a song in a bid to cheer* ZARA *up. She grabs her hand and they dance about the room. The beat* FATIMA *is listening to also becomes more intense.*

ALICE. Haram haram haram! Zara is haram! But she did the right thing, and didn't mean no harm. Haram, haram, haram haram haram!

They spin, getting faster and faster until it is too much. ZARA *flops to the floor, laughing.*

ZARA. I've created a monster!

ALICE (*suddenly worried*). You know I'm joking right? I'm not trying / to –

ZARA. Don't be silly. You say haram, I say Aryan witch.

ALICE *laughs. She checks* ZARA*'s plate.*

ALICE. You've left loads! Aryan witch demands you eat up!

ZARA. Can't! I'm stuffed. Such a fatty.

ALICE. It's just avocado and bread.

ZARA. Says the muesli fitness goddess!

ALICE. I had a doughnut too.

ZARA. What?

ALICE. ...And a few tablespoons of the vegan Ben & Jerry's. For breakfast. (*Appealing.*) It's tooooo good!

ZARA. Haha! Join me fellow fatttttyyyyy!

ZARA *opens her arms to* ALICE. ALICE *pretends to be unwilling, but then suddenly leaps onto* ZARA, *crushing her in a bear hug.* FATIMA *starts mouthing lyrics again. She misses a beat, swears.* LAYLA *calls to her from offstage. All bold italicised text is in Arabic.*

LAYLA (*offstage*). ***Fatima, is everything tidy in there?***

FATIMA. ***Yes, Mum.***

LAYLA (*offstage*). ***Zahra is supposed to arrive soon.***

FATIMA (*under her breath*). But we both know she'll be late.

LAYLA *enters, a beautiful and energetic woman.* FATIMA *scrabbles to hide what she's doing.* LAYLA *half-catches her.*

LAYLA. ***What are you doing?***

FATIMA. Nothing.

LAYLA (*handing* FATIMA *dishes to set the table*). ***Will you help me?***

FATIMA *helps* LAYLA *set the table. Meanwhile* ALICE *and* ZARA *cuddle like little kids, comfortable with each other.*

ZARA. God you weigh a ton.

ALICE. Shut up! My costume's gonna leave *very little* to the imagination, I can't feel fat! What are you wearing?

ZARA *hesitates*.

ZARA!

ZARA. You know I hate costumes!

ALICE. I don't care. We agreed white trash. Everyone's dressing up and you are no exception. (*At* ZARA*'s protest*.) Wear an old bra and some sweats and shut up. You don't get to be hot *all the time*!

ZARA. Screw you.

ALICE. Screw you too. Shall we get started then? Lots of cooking to –

ZARA*'s mobile rings again.* ALICE *is annoyed by it.*

Ugh! Again???

We see HUSSEIN *enter, on the phone. He's got a bit of a paunch. He is loud, playful, likes being the centre of attention. But he is also very generous and affectionate. Annoyed that nobody is answering, he hangs up. The buzzing stops.*

Phew!

HUSSEIN *dials a new number.* ZARA *and* ALICE's *house phone rings. They nearly jump out of their skins.*

What the fuck is that????

ZARA. House phone?

ALICE. We still have one of those?

LAYLA (*to* HUSSEIN). You are calling her?

HUSSEIN. Sh.

The girls try to find the house phone, but they don't know where it is, maybe it's buried under some papers or laundry. It goes to answerphone. HUSSEIN, *slightly annoyed, leaves a message.*

Zahra? Hello? Zahra, it is your baba. I am calling calling you but no reply. Do not forget you promise us to come to lunch today. Twelve thirty. We are waiting for you.

ZARA *realises she* has *forgotten. She mouths: 'shiiiiiiit' to* ALICE.

We have a news to tell you, darling, and your mother make kebab. So no excuse about work or this rubbish. Your mother she is missing you. I am missing you. Fatima too.

FATIMA *rolls her eyes.* ALICE *mouths an 'awww' to* ZARA.

Okay, we see you soon.

He hangs up.

LAYLA. She is coming?

HUSSEIN (*joking*). ***If she doesn't I will beat her!***

ZARA. Fuck.

ALICE. What's that all about? You come into some inheritance?

ZARA. Alice, my dad's an immigrant. And a cabbie. We don't get inheritances.

ALICE. You never know!

ZARA *stands*.

Where are you going?

ZARA. To have lunch with them? (*At* ALICE's *protests*.) Just for a couple of hours! Dad's right, I promised weeks ago. He even made me swear on the Prophet.

ALICE. I need you! Make an excuse!

ZARA. I'm out of excuses.

ALICE. Have you tried: 'I'm hungover'?

ZARA. As if! (*Impression of her father*.) 'What? You have been drinking? Shame on you!'

ALICE *joins in, doing the accent*.

ALICE. 'Dishonour!'

ZARA. 'A stain on the family!'

ALICE. 'Now go and marry your cousin!'

ALICE *folds over laughing*. ZARA *pauses, unsure if she is offended. Before she can decide*, ALICE *stops*.

Don't leave me. I can't be alone when people start arriving.

ZARA. I promise I'll be back quicker than you can say: 'awkward uni reunion'.

ALICE. It won't be awkward! Not if you're here.

ZARA. And I will be. In a couple of hours. There's no way I'd miss seeing Annabel's face when you tell her you've made partner. (*Hunting around the flat*.) Have you seen my boots anywhere?

ALICE. Under my jacket. You know Annabel runs her own business? Me being partner's hardly – I mean it's such a tiny law firm…

ZARA. Yeah. And I'm the intern.

ALICE (*correcting her*). Paralegal –

ZARA. Secretary at best.

It's awkward for a moment.

ALICE. Zara… are you sure it's not weird that I'll be –

ZARA. What?

ALICE. Well, your… (*Can't say it*.)

ZARA. Boss? Are you kidding? My whole life is you telling me what to do! It will just make work feel like home.

ALICE. Cow! I'll have you know I'm assertive, not bossy!

ZARA. But of *course*. Look, you don't have to play it down for me. It's a great achievement, and I'm really proud of you.

ALICE.…Thank you. (*Beat*.) Annabel's also getting married next year… And Mia's engaged…

ZARA. So? You're crushing your career.

ALICE. I know, but…

ZARA. I thought men weren't important.

ALICE. They're not. Doesn't mean they're not allowed to propose to me… Speaking of proposals, I've got one for you –

ZARA. – I love you but unfortunately I'm straight.

ALICE. No. Anthony… I'd like to ask him to move in. What do you think?

ZARA.…Oh. Is that not a bit… soon?

ALICE. Maybe… (*This tumbles out, a guilty confession*.) Actually, I'm really sorry, I might have already asked him. And he might have said… YES!!!! I know, it's a bit sudden, and I should have asked you, but first it was like, Zara's getting married and leaving *anyway*, and then it was like, oh fuck she's gonna break up with Jamil, she's got too much on her plate right now… and *then* last night I was lying there with Anthony, thinking: Yes, maybe he's not the erudite, successful *genius* I pictured myself with. But he's gorgeous, and sexy, and nice! And he actually *makes* me cum, I mean like I don't have to think about something else, Anthony just makes it happen, which okay, is not the most traditional thing to base a relationship on but fucking hell it's rare, am I right?

ZARA. Um, yeah. It's pretty… rare.

ALICE. Exactly. And that body – well a girl would travel a long way for that body… (*Beat. Genuine.*) I'm sorry. I should have talked to you. If you hate the idea, I will of course tell him to fuck off. Because you are my wife. First and foremost. You know that.

ZARA. It's your house, Alice.

ALICE. It's both of ours…

ZARA. It's the house your dad bought for you. (*Regrets how that came out.*) I mean, you should do what you want.

ALICE. Do you hate the idea of him living here?

ZARA. Course I don't hate it…

ALICE. But it's weird? He's coming tonight, meeting everyone. You could chat, get to know each other better, see how you feel…?

ZARA's mobile rings again, giving her an escape.

ZARA. Shit. Probably my dad again. I'd better get going.

ALICE. Stay. Talk to me –

ZARA (*finding her boots in a pile of clothes*). I can't. I haven't visited for like four months.

ALICE. So what? I only see mine at Christmas.

ZARA. Four months is like four years to them.

ALICE. Lucky girl. To have them love you so much. (*At ZARA's sarcastic face.*) Fine. Go. But text me. Text me or I'll send you tit pics in front of your dad.

ZARA. I promise!

ALICE. Are you going to tell them about Jamil?

ZARA. I don't know.

ALICE. You have to. Before they hear it from someone else.

ZARA. Yes, Mummy.

ALICE. And no fake praying! Just tell them you're a heathen!

ZARA. No way.

She pulls on a coat. ALICE *suddenly has brainwave.*

ALICE. Wait, I've got it: 'A Heathen in Hiding – The Life and Times of Zara Al-Attas'.

ZARA. You're a dick.

ZARA exits. ALICE *sighs, alone with a lot of cleaning and prep to do.*

2. Saturday lunchtime

FATIMA, *carrying plates, lets* ZARA *in.*

FATIMA. You're late.

ZARA. Hi Fatti, nice to see you too.

FATIMA. Don't call me that.

ZARA. What? It's your name, *ain't* it?

FATIMA. No. It *ain't.*

ZARA. Where's Mum?

FATIMA. Cooking. You got pissed last night.

ZARA.…What? No I di–

FATIMA. You smell weird. And your eyes are bloodshot.

ZARA. I just slept badly.

FATIMA. Whatever.

ZARA. How's college?

FATIMA. Dry.

ZARA. Got a boyfriend?

FATIMA. Don't be stupid.

ZARA. Your hair looks nice. Who did it like that?

FATIMA. Keisha.

ZARA (*enthusiastic*). Oh, great, is Keisha your friend?

FATIMA. No.

ZARA....Cool. (*Beat.*) Well it's good to see you...

FATIMA *kisses her teeth and moves to exit to the kitchen.*

FATIMA. At least chew some gum before you talk to Baba. Your breath stinks – Mama! Zahra's here!

FATIMA *exits.* ZARA *tries to ignore her comment but then pops a piece of gum in her mouth – just in case.*

LAYLA *enters. She's been washing up. Her sleeves are pulled up and her forearms are wet. A pause while* LAYLA *looks at her daughter, takes her in.*

LAYLA. Zahra. *My baby.*

LAYLA *hugs* ZARA. *A heartfelt embrace that says the things she can't put into words. It is a little too much for* ZARA. *Eventually* LAYLA *breaks away, chatting in Arabic excitedly.*

Don't let it be this long again! Five – six months? It's too much! How are you? You must have so much to tell me – the wedding!

ZARA *dithers. She hasn't fully understood her mother's Arabic at that pace.* LAYLA *pauses, confused.*

Zahra?

ZARA. Sorry, I'm just a bit... haven't spoken Arabic in a while...

LAYLA. You forget?

ZARA. No, no! Just, can you say that slower?

LAYLA. You forget because you never visiting! We have not seen you for six month!

ZARA. It's not that long! Four, / five max –

LAYLA. Six month. (*A beat. Grins.*) No problem, I practise my English with you.

ZARA. No, no, I'll understand if –

LAYLA. Zahra, please. I never have the chance to practise! So... (*In her best English.*) How-is-your-wedding-planning-going?

ZARA. Look, I brought you these.

ZARA hands LAYLA some cheap, slightly wilted flowers from the corner shop. An afterthought on the way. Handing them over, she realises how rubbish they are. LAYLA is gracious, but slightly confused by the gift.

I thought you could... put them on the windowsill or something.

LAYLA. Darling, this is your home. You don't need to bring us gift.

ZARA (*taking off her coat*). It's boiling in here. Is the heating on?

LAYLA. I think yes.

ZARA. In May? (*Noticing LAYLA staring.*) What?

LAYLA. You are looking... different.

Before ZARA can respond, HUSSEIN's voice booms from offstage.

HUSSEIN. YA, WOMAN! *I marry you because I thought you could cook. All I smell is burning!*

LAYLA. I greet our daughter, Hussein! (*To ZARA.*) Men! What is it, darling?

ZARA. I – Has he always called you 'woman'?

LAYLA. Only when he is hungry! Why?

ZARA. No, nothing. I just never –

HUSSEIN *enters*.

HUSSEIN. My girl!

HUSSEIN *almost sweeps* ZARA *off her feet, pulling her into a tight embrace as if she is a small child.* ZARA *squirms.* HUSSEIN *pulls away, playfully chastising* ZARA.

I should be beating you, not embracing you! Never answering your phone!

LAYLA. Hussein. **English. Zahra does not understand.**

HUSSEIN. **What? Of course she / does!**

LAYLA (*with a smile, but firm*). *English.* We will all practise.

HUSSEIN *is confused for a minute but quickly recovers. He grabs* ZARA *by the wrists and assesses her. She wriggles uncomfortably.* FATIMA *comes back with more plates. She and* LAYLA *set the table.*

HUSSEIN. British girl, eh? (*Disapproving.*) Your clothing very tight.

ZARA. Sorry, Dad. It's probably coz I've put on / weight –

HUSSEIN. No. Very skinny. You are going to the gym? Getting ready for wedding photo?

ZARA. Er… yeah. Something like / that…

HUSSEIN. See, Fatima? Your sister is doing exercise. That is why she is looking like a supermodel!

FATIMA. Whatever.

ZARA. I don't look like a supermodel, / Dad –

HUSSEIN (*to* FATIMA). *You* are eating like a donkey and then complaining!

LAYLA. Hussein, leave her.

FATIMA. Least I ain't as fat as you, Baba!

HUSSEIN. Your baba is allowed to be fat. It is not good on a woman. (*To* ZARA.) But be careful, my girl. I think *this* is too thin – how you will have children? Poor Jamil.

ZARA. Can't win with you, Dad!

HUSSEIN. Ya, see your mother, she has perfect amount.
Enough to hold!

> HUSSEIN *grabs* LAYLA *by the waist, she screams,*
> *laughing.* FATIMA *starts sneaking away upstairs.*

LAYLA. Wicked man! *You* keep me in good shape, always
running everywhere for you. (*To* FATIMA.) ***Can you help
me, Fatima?***

FATIMA. Ah, man, can't I just... (*Stops herself.*) Sorry, Mama.
Of course.

> FATIMA *exits with* LAYLA. ZARA *feels awkward alone*
> *with her dad.*

ZARA. Is Fatima all right?

HUSSEIN. She is fine, fine. But her grades is very bad.

ZARA (*shocked*). What? Really?

HUSSEIN. Yes. Is a shame, she is not very intelligent. Not like
you. She getting grade two, three in everything... I say to her,
'What is two? Is it like B?' She say 'No, is like F!' Then she is
complaining to be on diet, but eating everything in the house!
Like me! This country a wicked place, Zahra. Everywhere
there is sweets. Back home in the village I never have this
problem. We are always walking, running with the sheeps – no
need for gym! But here in UK, driving all day on my bottom,
the office biscuit tin – (*Patting tummy.*) Is dangerous!

ZARA. Biscuit tin?

HUSSEIN. New operator, Sandra. Ya, she is trouble! She is
making all the drivers give to her 'kitty', then she buy
biscuit. I like custard creams too too much. *Mashallah*, I am
getting a very big belly.

ZARA (*amused despite herself*). Do some exercise, Dad!

HUSSEIN. When I do? I work morning evening night, darling.

> *Now they're alone,* ZARA *leans in, confidential.*

ZARA. How's business going?

HUSSEIN (*batting off her concern*). Fine, fine.

ZARA. You sure? Coz I'm happy to –

HUSSEIN. What is this? A man cannot provide?

ZARA. Just… if things get… difficult again…

HUSSEIN (*firm*). They will not. I always take care this family, Zahra… (*Suddenly loud, playful.*) So my girls can have everything they want! iPad for your sister, furniture for your mother! They work me like donkey!

LAYLA *enters again during this last sentence, carrying the flowers in a gaudy vase.*

LAYLA. What you are saying, you terrible man?

HUSSEIN (*kissing her*). I am saying how lucky I am to have a beautiful wife!

LAYLA. Hmmm.

LAYLA *places the flowers on the centre of the table with a flourish – a sad wilted sight.* ZARA*'s embarrassed.*

ZARA. Aw, Mum, you didn't have to –

LAYLA. They are very beautiful.

HUSSEIN. Yes. And today we want to be *special*. Where is Jamil?

ZARA.…Jamil?

LAYLA. We are thinking you will bring him.

ZARA. Oh. Um… I thought it was just family.

HUSSEIN. He *is* family! Silly girl! Ya, Layla, phone Amira and tell her send my son-in-law for / dinner!

ZARA (*too loud*). NO! (*Recovering.*) No, he's um… working, today.

HUSSEIN. On the weekend?

ZARA. Yeah.

HUSSEIN. Good boy. I like this. Providing for my daughter! So? Why we have not seen you so long? Amira giving you hard time with wedding planning? She is like dragon, Amira.

LAYLA. Hussein!

HUSSEIN. Layla, she is! I just thanking God I raise a strong woman that can handle this mother-in-law!

ZARA. ...How comes we're using the table?

HUSSEIN. Ah. For you, darling. We know you like.

ZARA. I don't mind the floor –

LAYLA. Remember when you are a little girl? You love to eat on this table. You like / to –

HUSSEIN (*barrelling over*). You make us pretend we are in the restaurant, you are the... waitress. You...

ZARA (*who has heard this many times*). Dad –

HUSSEIN. You write us small menu, you folding toilet paper everywhere, one hundred knife, fork spoon. Tie a cloths here. (*Indicates an apron.*) You pick up the bowl, *Mashallah* is bigger than your head. We say 'Zahra, you are too young, let Mama do it, please!' But you become so angry. We have no choice. We say: 'We have to let this girl do what she wants!'

In the flat, ALICE *enters, carrying a huge pot. She staggers under its weight.*

LAYLA. – She is very stubborn, like her father!

HUSSEIN. So we watching you very carefully –

LAYLA. The pot very heavy and you are very small –

HUSSEIN. You are walking too-too slow. (*Does an impression.*) Finally you are nearly reaching table. We make thanks to God, it will be okay. And then, ouf!

ALICE *drops the pot with a loud clang, it lands on her foot. She swears.*

You fall! Food everywhere. On the carpet. The chairs. Even the ceiling!

ALICE *is fuming.* HUSSEIN *finds his story very funny.* ZARA *less so, but she laughs politely.* LAYLA *watches her.*

LAYLA. You cry so much.

HUSSEIN. We never do restaurant table again!

FATIMA *comes in, wearing a headscarf.*

FATIMA. Baba! It's *Dhuhr.*

HUSSEIN. Ah! (*To* ZARA.) You are coming to pray?

ZARA. Um… Yeah. Yeah of course.

HUSSEIN. Get your sister a scarf, Fatima.

FATIMA *grabs a scarf from the side and chucks it at* ZARA, *scowling suspiciously.*

Layla?

LAYLA. I have done already. *Yallah*, hurry. Go before the food is cold!

HUSSEIN *and* FATIMA *leave.* ZARA *stays a beat longer.* ALICE *flops on the floor, fed up, nursing her bruised foot.*

ZARA. Do you need some help?

LAYLA. No no. You can join them.

ZARA. I don't…

ZARA *trails off.* LAYLA *smiles at her knowingly.*

LAYLA. Then rest. You have travelled far.

ZARA. Oh, it's not that f–

LAYLA. You tell me it take ninety minutes to get here, that is why you cannot visit after work.

ZARA (*caught out*). Oh… Yeah, yeah. I mean it's long. But it's not…

LAYLA. Sit. Talk to me.

ZARA *sits awkwardly.* LAYLA *continues setting the table. Pissed off,* ALICE *takes out her phone and shoves it down her top. She takes a picture and sends it to* ZARA.

Your job is good?

ALICE (*texting aloud*). Come the fuck back!

ZARA. Um… yeah. Yeah, alright.

ZARA's phone beeps and she reads the text from ALICE, *tries not to laugh. She starts to reply.* LAYLA *waits for more detail but it doesn't come.*

LAYLA. Your friend she is well?

ZARA (*not looking up*). Mmm.

LAYLA. What her name is again?

ZARA. Yeah.

LAYLA. What. Is. Her. Name?

ZARA. Huh? Oh. Alice. Alice.

ZARA sends a message. ALICE *reads it, laughs, texts back.*

ALICE. They are NOT saggy. Bitch!

LAYLA. How is she?

ZARA. She's good.

ZARA snorts at ALICE's *text.* LAYLA *waits for a proper response. Eventually* ZARA *notices, puts her phone down.*

…She just got promoted. She's going to be a partner. At the firm we both work at.

LAYLA. Ah! Congratulation! She is happy?

ZARA. Yes, very. (*Sudden thought.*) Actually, we're having a party tonight, so I can't stay too –

ALICE, *on the other side of the space, picks up a hipster Middle-Eastern recipe book. It totally confuses her.*

LAYLA. And you?

ZARA. Me? (*Frustrated that* LAYLA *hasn't understood.*) No, *I* didn't make partner. *Alice* did.

LAYLA. No. Are you happy?

ZARA. Oh. Yes I'm fine. (*At her mother's face.*) I'm very well, Mum.

ALICE *texts* ZARA *again.* ZARA's *phone buzzes.* ZARA *nearly picks it up, but clocking* LAYLA's *face, she stops.*

ALICE. Text back, I need you!

LAYLA. Work is good?

ZARA. Yeah. Just busy.

ALICE (*texting*). What is baba ganoush? Can you ask your mum how to make it?

LAYLA. And Jamil? You are excited to / be –

ZARA. – Is this new?

ZARA *points at the floor.* LAYLA *looks at* ZARA, *deciding whether to let her divert. She concedes.*

LAYLA. Yes. I lie this myself.

ZARA. On your own?!

LAYLA. Yes.

ZARA. Mum!

LAYLA. Ouf, this is nothing. My body is strong, it take a lot!

ALICE *starts really struggling, making a mess with pots, aubergine, etc.*

ZARA. But the doctors said you should…

LAYLA. No. To rest is to let pain win. When I feel pain, I say to myself: 'Layla, it is there – (*Gestures away from her body.*) you are here.' Pain is not inside me. It is separate.

ZARA. 'The Pain is Separate – Tales from a Refugee Survivor'.

LAYLA. What?

ZARA. Sorry, it's a game me and Alice play. Find a title for your autobiography.

LAYLA. I am not refugee any more.

ZARA. Yeah, but immigrant wouldn't sell as well.

LAYLA (*firm*). I am British citizen now.

ZARA *is surprised by* LAYLA*'s reaction. A tense beat. In the other space,* ALICE *is getting frustrated. She texts* ZARA *again.* ZARA *ignores the buzz.*

LAYLA. Zahra… can I talk with you?

ALICE. Fuck this.

   ALICE *goes out, slamming the door.*

ZARA. We're talking now…

LAYLA. I mean the proper way… Zahra, are you –

HUSSEIN (*offstage*). ZAHRA!! YOU ARE COMING?

   ZARA *looks at her mother expectantly.*

LAYLA (*with a sigh*). Go, he is waiting.

   ZARA *grabs the headscarf and leaves.*

3. Early Saturday evening

ALICE *re-enters with bags of packaged food from a posh deli.
She sets the packets on the table. Overstressed, she yanks open
a tub and spills it down her top, swears.* ZARA *appears
carrying shopping bags. She looks exhausted, broken. But the
second* ALICE *spots her she collects herself, hiding her feelings
so proficiently it's like they were never there.*

ALICE. Thank fucking God! Baba ganoush?

ZARA. What?

ALICE. Baba ganoush! I text you asking to get the recipe from
   your mum!

ZARA. Oh… sorry.

ALICE. I can't cook, mine's a mess! Fix it please! And can you
   lay those out? I've got to change my top.

   ALICE *exits,* ZARA*'s alone. She begins to open the packets
   of food. Meanwhile, on the other side,* LAYLA *has finished
   preparing the table. The rest of the family enter to take their
   seats at the dinner table.* HUSSEIN *calls out to* ZARA.

4. Saturday lunch, a little after Scene Two

HUSSEIN. Zahra!

> ZARA *comes over, headscarf in her hands.*

> You take a long time. Much to pray for, huh?

ZARA. Um, where do I put –

> FATIMA *snatches the scarf from* ZARA *and puts it to the side.* FATIMA *keeps her headscarf on.* ZARA *stares at it.*

> Aren't you taking yours… [off]?

FATIMA. No. I like it.

LAYLA. Sit. Eat.

> ZARA *sits at the table and the family begin to eat.* HUSSEIN *sits in the centre.* FATIMA *is surreptitiously on her iPad.* LAYLA *busies herself serving people. The meal is huge, countless dishes. Everyone munches heartily, dipping their bread into the food.* ZARA *is the only one using a knife and fork.*

> Zahra, you want couscous?

ZARA. It's okay, I'll do it.

> ZARA *puts a very small amount of couscous on her plate. The family watch with curiosity. Eventually* HUSSEIN *becomes impatient. He grabs* ZARA*'s plate and doles food onto it.*

> Dad!

HUSSEIN (*joking*). *Ya, donkey! You cannot eat just salad.*

LAYLA. Hussein, no Arabic!

FATIMA. Yeah, Zahra's too English to speak our language now.

ZARA. Don't be ridiculous.

FATIMA. 'Ridiculous'. You sound so white!

ZARA. This is how everyone talks. We can't all be faux-hoodrats.

FATIMA. How am I a hoodrat? This is my / voice –

HUSSEIN. Fatima, don't be jealous! Our Zahra, she speak English like the Queen! (*Patting* ZARA*'s head proudly.*) My clever daughter, bachelor degree! First in our family.

FATIMA (*to* ZARA). What was it you got again? A / third?

HUSSEIN. Ya, I am very proud of my girl. A lawyer! You know without lawyer your baba would not be allow stay here, not your mother either…

ZARA. Yeah. I mean that's immigration law, Dad, and I would love to do that one day but I'm not even a qualified solicitor yet –

HUSSEIN. My daughter is immigration lawyer! (*To* FATIMA.) See you could be like this, becoming doctor, helping people, but you are lazier than donkey!

FATIMA. Baba! I wanted to be doctor when I was five. I told you, I'm gonna start my own / business –

HUSSEIN. Fatima! To heal sick people, or to help people who are refugee, what is more better than this?! My girls can do anything! The world is different place now, women even fighting terrorist. You should have a big dreams. Not driving these rude, dangerous people one side of London to other. I will not allow.

LAYLA. *Alhamdulillah.*

FATIMA. But –

HUSSEIN. No, Fatima. I will not allow.

FATIMA *sulks.*

LAYLA (*to* FATIMA). Darling, it is too dangerous. I even wish for your father to stop driving.

HUSSEIN. What can I do, woman? You want to starve?

LAYLA. No, I want my husband to be safe! Zahra, this week one boy –

HUSSEIN. Yes. A boy, he comes with this white powder, this sniff-sniff for the nose? I say to him 'Mate, not in my cab.' The language he is using to me, very bad, I will not repeat.

LAYLA. No, don't repeat.

HUSSEIN. He insist to stop in Camden. I am waiting twenty minutes. He go inside and come back with a big bag of this stuffs. I tell him 'Mate, this is not okay, I did not agree this.' He tells him shut up. He holds knife to me. I say, 'Please mate, I have two daughters.' I will not lie, my girls, I am frighten.

He laugh. Then police car coming so he run. He do not pay me. A black boy.

LAYLA *tuts, shakes her head in sympathy.* ZARA *struggles. She decides to address this.*

ZARA. Dad... why is it important he was black?

HUSSEIN. What?

ZARA. You shouldn't just... you shouldn't say he was black like that.

HUSSEIN. I am not making judgement, Zahra. I am saying truth. This black boy do not pay for his cab.

ZARA. But his colour isn't the *reason* he didn't –

HUSSEIN. Black boys they do this!

ZARA. Dad!

FATIMA. He don't mean it like that, man, calm down.

HUSSEIN. What is problem? I am just saying his colour. I will say it if he is black white orange green –

ZARA. You should be careful. About sounding...

HUSSEIN (*irritated now*). He was black boy! I am telling you he threatened your baba life and you are upset because I say the colour of his skin? This pig in my car call me terrorist!

A slightly awkward silence. LAYLA *takes* HUSSEIN's *hand, a supportive and calming gesture. He looks at her.*

Anyway, what I *try* to say, is Fatima should not be driving cabs. She should study to be doctor.

ZARA. I agree. You're smarter than that!

FATIMA. What do you know?

HUSSEIN. Good. Then you see I am right.

LAYLA. Everyone is happy.

FATIMA. Not me!

LAYLA. *Yallah*, eat! Zahra, you do not hardly touch! You do not like my cooking?

FATIMA. She probably only eats like pulled-pork sweet-potato wraps now.

HUSSEIN. Pork? My girl does not eat pork, Fatima!

ZARA. No I don't. I'm fine, Mum, honestly. It's just, I'm trying veganism?

The whole family reacts.

LAYLA. Viganizzm?

ZARA. Yeah, it's… more environmental, and healthy…

HUSSEIN. What is vegan?

FATIMA. It's dumb, Baba. They can't eat nothing.

ZARA. Course we can eat. Just not meat, eggs, or dairy.

HUSSEIN. WHAT? *Majnuna!*

LAYLA. You can eat this?

ZARA. Yes. That's a salad.

HUSSEIN (*indicating a dish*). This?

ZARA. Yes Dad, that's baba ganoush.

HUSSEIN. This?

ZARA (*trying to stay patient*). Yep, that's hummus. Vegans live off hummus.

FATIMA. Colonialism.

ZARA. *What?*

FATIMA. Colonialism. White vegans appropriate our culture and our food. Halloumi fries and that.

ZARA. Halloumi's from Cyprus and it isn't vegan!

LAYLA. I make you lentil soup, Zahra? Or fasoulia?

ZARA. Honestly I'm fine.

LAYLA. Yoghurt...?

ZARA (*a little too firm*). No! Thank you. Please, don't worry, I'll eat whatever you give me.

HUSSEIN. Good! Then have kebab.

He dishes meat onto her plate. ZARA *tries to hide her disgust.*

I will tell Jamil to stop this viganissim. Kebab is healthy, darling! You need strong body. Nobody will come to your wedding if you do not give them meat! Ya, you should let your mother to cook. Then your guests will be happy!

LAYLA. Yes I can do! Fatima will help.

FATIMA *stifles a protest.*

ZARA. Oh no, I couldn't ask that of you –

LAYLA. I do not mind! What about henna party? You plan this yet?

HUSSEIN. You will have cake? I know good place you can buy in Edgware Road.

LAYLA. And dresses? You have them yet? I can come with you to shopping...

FATIMA (*smirking*). A white dress, yeah?

ZARA. I don't... I don't have dresses yet. Or a cake. But I'm not –

HUSSEIN (*horrified*). *Ya – Allah!* WHY?

LAYLA. Something happen, Zahra? With Jamil?

A pause. Now would be the time to tell them. Suddenly there is a loud bang outside. They all jump.

FATIMA. FUCK!

Dogs begin barking outside.

LAYLA. Don't swear, Fatima.

HUSSEIN (*going to the window*). It's those boys. WE WILL
CATCH YOU! YOU ARE NOT CLEVER!

*There are shouts back from outside. Enraged, HUSSEIN
begins to head for the door.*

LAYLA. Hussein! Do not go outside! It is dangerous.

*But HUSSEIN has exited onto the estate walkway, still
yelling at the boys below.*

HUSSEIN (*offstage*). You bastard boys! I will teach you to
make trouble for my family!

*LAYLA is very anxious. FATIMA peers out the window,
badly hiding her excitement at the drama.*

FATIMA. I'm gonna go see what he's doing. It's just dumb
kids, Mama. It's safe!

LAYLA. These kids carrying knifes, Fatima!

*But FATIMA is gone too. LAYLA cries out, exasperated.
A pause.*

ZARA.... You okay, Mum?

LAYLA. There is nothing more stupid than a man with hurt
pride, Zahra, nothing.

*ZARA hovers, unsure of the best way to comfort LAYLA.
We hear HUSSEIN's shouts offstage.*

5. Early Saturday evening, just after Scene Three

On the other side of the space, ALICE *re-enters in a clean top.*

ALICE. So? Did you fix it?

> ZARA, *still hovering between worlds, is caught out. She wipes her face.*

ZARA. Not really… I don't know how to make baba ganoush.

ALICE. What? What kind of Arab are you?

ZARA (*holding up her shopping*). The best kind. The kind that brings lots of wine.

ALICE. Yes! My hero!… Wait: 'Haram Hero – A Millennial Memoir'.

ZARA.…Good one.

ALICE. What did you get?

ZARA. White and red. Four forty-nine. God I love Lidl. And I got those fake Pringles you like. And jelly babies.

ALICE. Oh.

ZARA. What?

ALICE. I think… the guys will want something more… classy?

ZARA. Classy? Since when? I've seen Michael down an entire Lambrini!

ALICE. When we were *students*! He owns a Chateau in France now, Zara!

> *Beat.*

ZARA. Right. Okay. I'll pop out. You mean like a tenner a bottle?

ALICE.…More? Do you have enough money? I'll give / you –

ZARA. Don't be stupid.

ALICE. I've got loads in my wallet…

ZARA. Alice. I can afford a bottle of wine.

> ZARA *starts to go.* ALICE *feels desperately awkward.*

ALICE. You know what, leave it. I told everyone to bring their own anyway. And people will love Lidl. They'll think it's nostalgic. Honestly.

ALICE lays the bottles down, and finishes opening the numerous posh snacks ZARA started unwrapping in Scene Three.

ZARA. Sure you got enough?

ALICE. Great, aren't they? All gluten-free and vegan – I went to that new deli –

ZARA. Alice! We're boycotting them. Mr Singh said he's gonna have to shut down coz of that place.

ALICE. Mr Singh still doesn't have cashew milk.

ZARA. They're not actually independent you know. They're a big chain masquerading as a local.

ALICE. I'll accept that argument from you when you stop using Uber. Try some?

ZARA. Oh. No thanks. Huge lunch.

ALICE. Lunch was hours ago!

ZARA. Yeah but you know what they're like. (*In Arabic accent.*) 'Eat, darling, / eat, eat.'

At the same time LAYLA, who is sat alone, stands and calls out to her family.

LAYLA. *Please*, come back to eat!

ALICE. Wait, I've got a surprise.

ALICE turns away. ZARA stares at her mother, lost in thought. ALICE turns back with a bottle of vintage champagne.

Dad got it for me, as a congratulations present. Buying my love as usual, but never mind. Come on, before everyone gets here.

ZARA. Oh… I might not tonight…

ALICE. What???

ZARA. I just feel a bit…

ALICE. No way! Absolutely not. Fuck that.

She pops the bottle expertly and begins to pour glasses.
ZARA watches, a feeling of foreboding as the glasses fill.

ZARA. Remember when I didn't drink?

ALICE. Yeah. You were boring as fuck – I'm kidding! Look,
fuck families, fuck exes, fuck sobriety, here's to us! (*Hands
her a glass.*) Did you tell your parents? About Jamil?

ZARA. Um… yeah.

ALICE (*with concern*). And did they…?

ZARA (*raising her glass*). To us!

ALICE. Yes! Us! (*Clinking glasses.*) Tonight's gonna be great.
I can feel it. For you especially. (*Pointed.*) Did you know
Michael runs his own firm now?

ZARA. And?

ALICE. He's always had a soft spot for / you…

ZARA. No, Alice.

ALICE. Why not?

ZARA. Coz! I'm not even technically –

ALICE. He'd probably pay for you to finish your LPC, you
know. He'd probably pay you just to *stand* there. He'd
probably pay you for…

She waggles her eyebrows. ZARA laughs.

ZARA. You are so gross!

ALICE (*serious*). I just think it could be a good solution. You
know I'm your number-one fan. And you deserve to be in
those rooms. You ARE good enough. You are an incredible,
talented, intelligent woman. Something is coming, I feel it!
(*Holding her stomach.*) Here.

ZARA. That's gas.

ALICE. Promise you'll talk to him about it, pleaaaaaaaaaaase?

ZARA. Fine, whatever.

ALICE. YES! To us!

ZARA. To us!

> *They drink. Meanwhile,* FATIMA *re-enters from outside, with a pissed-off* HUSSEIN *behind her.*

(*To* ALICE.) Please, don't let me get wasted / tonight.

FATIMA. Rah! They were proper wasted, Mama.

6. Saturday lunch, just after Scene Four

FATIMA *relays the story to her family, enjoying the drama but trying to remain respectful.* ZARA *is drawn over.*

FATIMA. They got cannies and they're all like, 'Shut up bin Laden' – and Baba was like, 'I will teach you discipline, your mother would be ASHAMED', so then the big one, he goes: 'What you say about my mum? I got a strap, you dickh–' (*Correcting herself for* LAYLA.) 'You idiot!'

But Baba don't know what a strap is, innit, he thinks it's a belt, and I know Dean, Dean ain't got no strap, he used to be in top set for maths, but Baba's going, 'I have many straps too, you come up here and I will show you what I will do with my strap!' so then one of them takes his dog off the lead innit, and he's shouting: 'Go get him AK' – what kind of name is AK for a dog anyway? – and then the dog starts barking proper loud and Baba jumps so they all start laughing – (*Sensing the atmosphere.*) and then they walked off, a bit down the road.

> *Silence.* HUSSEIN *is seething.* LAYLA *looks at him with concern.*

LAYLA. The car is okay?

HUSSEIN. Yes is fine. I check when they leave. They put firework underneath again but luckily no damage.

ZARA. You should call the police, Dad.

FATIMA. Police only help white people. (*At* ZARA*'s face.*) It's true. Even Baba thinks so. Innit, Baba?

HUSSEIN *just sighs.*

HUSSEIN. The sooner we are leaving the better. Everywhere outside there is shits from their dogs, Layla.

LAYLA. Hussein, don't / swear.

ZARA. You *can* report that, Dad.

HUSSEIN. Zahra, when I call council, a man comes and I see him stroking these disgusting animals. He tell me they are 'harmless pet'. Why the English love dogs so much?

FATIMA. Because they're all nuts.

ZARA. You can't call a whole country of people nuts.

FATIMA. I can if they are.

HUSSEIN. Picking up animal's mess from the street. Letting it lick your face. It is disgusting. Dogs are a weapon. These people have short memory but I don't forget. Soldiers use them. Police use them. And now these stupid boys use them to scare us in our own home.

LAYLA. Come and eat, *Yallah*.

HUSSEIN. The English treat their dogs better than us. It is true. I don't want to be in this neighbourhood any more. It break my heart. Is nothing but pimp, gangster...

FATIMA. And hipsters. Guess your mates wanna be near their dealers, innit.

ZARA. They're not *my* / mates...

HUSSEIN. All our friends are gone, Zahra, move to better area. I miss my community. And these teenage boys stand outside making a trouble. I am worried for the safety of your sister.

ZARA. FATTI?!

HUSSEIN *looks at* LAYLA.

HUSSEIN. *I am going to do it now, Layla.*

LAYLA….Now? *Is now a good time, / darling?*

HUSSEIN (*standing up*). I would like to make announcement.

FATIMA (*to* ZARA). I told you not to call me Fatti, dickhead.

HUSSEIN. Girls…

ZARA. See what I mean? *Fatti* can take care of herself!

LAYLA. Girls, your baba would like to –

FATIMA. I swear down, one more time…

HUSSEIN. Girls! ENOUGH.

Beat. The girls shut up.

Zahra, we have a good news. We are going to buy a house. (*Dramatic pause*.)…In Brent.

Pause. ZARA just stares.

LAYLA. It is wonderful, yes?

ZARA. Um. Yeah. Sorry, Brent?

HUSSEIN. Everyone is there now. All our friends –

LAYLA. Muhammed and Mariam. Abdullah's family… of course Amira and / Jamil…

HUSSEIN. We find perfect house with three bedrooms, Zahra. And garden! I am going to plant… fig tree. Like when I was a boy.

ZARA. Why didn't you tell me?

HUSSEIN. *Ya kelb*. I call you every day! You don't answer.

FATIMA. You never do.

LAYLA. Your father has dream to own somewhere ever since we arrive in England…

FATIMA. I can't wait, man. You should see the room I'll have. It's twice as big, nah nah, THREE times as big, Baba says I can get my own TV in there –

ZARA. How are you going to afford it?

A shared look between the parents.

LAYLA. Jamil *really* never tell you?

HUSSEIN. He want us to surprise her, darling.

LAYLA. I know this, but –

ZARA. What's Jamil got to do with the –

HUSSEIN. Ah! (*Enjoying the story.*) See, I complain to Amira about this area. She tell me: 'Come to Brent!' So we looking, but expensive!

LAYLA. Then Jamil approach your father. You know, if you live in council house for long time, / they –

HUSSEIN. Yes, the council give you big discount to buy it. We have been here now twenty-five…?

LAYLA. Twenty-six / years –

HUSSEIN. So we have very big discount, *if* we want to buy this horrible place. Of course, we don't. But Jamil, he is clever. He come to me, he say: 'Uncle, I want your flat. I will pay you to buy it with your discount, and I will give you extra twenty per cent on top. This you can use this for deposit in Brent, pay me back whenever you are ready… without interest, because we are family!'

ZARA. I don't understand –

HUSSEIN (*rolling eyes*). Ouf, your mother is confused too! Listen, Jamil he give me the money, I buy this flat, I sign over to him. Jamil get discount property in London, and we get big house in Brent. *Khalas*. Ya, estate agents is very clever, / Zahra!

ZARA. Jamil wants to live *here*?

HUSSEIN (*laughing*). No, *ya majnuna*! *Nobody* want to live here! He is buying for investment. He will rent. He tell me these students, they will pay one thousand, even two thousand rent for two-bedroom flat in this area.

FATIMA. Told you, English people are crazy.

Beat. ZARA is reeling. This is a really big mess. Fuck.

LAYLA (*with concern*). What you are thinking, Zahra?

ZARA. You decided all this together?

HUSSEIN. Yes, few months ago.

ZARA. But didn't think to ask me?

HUSSEIN. Why I should ask? Is business deal between me and Jamil.

ZARA *needs to find a way out of this. She realises something.*

ZARA. Coz it's illegal.

LAYLA (*anxious*). Illegal?

ZARA (*to* LAYLA). Yes. To buy a council flat for someone else. To use your discount if it won't be *your* home.

HUSSEIN (*dismissive*). Ouf!

ZARA. I'm serious. There's huge *lists* of people who need council flats. If you get caught…

HUSSEIN. This list! We know this list well. Because of list we spend two years in B&B with rats! Zahra, the only people council help are drug dealers, criminals, and homeless.

FATIMA. Everyone lies, man. Khadija at school, her big sister pretended she was gay and said her parents kicked her out, now she's got a flat in Archway and she's gonna move in with her boyfriend.

ZARA. That's nonsense!

FATIMA. No it ain't, ask Khadija.

LAYLA. Ya, Hussein, maybe Zahra is right.

HUSSEIN (*laughing*). It is reason like this women should not do business.

ZARA. Says the man who can barely run his.

HUSSEIN.…What?

ZARA. I just mean… You were *given* this. You were lucky. England didn't *have* to do that and you shouldn't… take too much –

HUSSEIN. Too much? Zahra, when we arrive, nearly dead, this government give us as little as possible. Enough to keep us alive, *bas*. We are very grateful then. Nobody is shooting us, you are safe, we get your mother to doctor. But I pay this country back, Zahra! Double, three times I pay. I work every day. When I fall on hard time, I never stop. I give my rents, my taxes, I don't take benefit! Never. I don't go to hospital, even when I am ill! My children have a British passport, they go to British school and still people treat us like we are dirtier than the bags of shits they carry for their dogs. I am suppose to be grateful forever? Maybe it is a small breaking of law… (*At* LAYLA's *protest, firm.*) a small one, Layla, but is nothing compare to what they do to us. Nowadays they just leaving people like us, women, children, young men leave us to drown in boats, wash up on seashore. I owe Britain nothing.

A pause. What can ZARA *say now? She takes a deep breath.* LAYLA *watches her daughter with concern.*

ZARA. You can't let Jamil buy this flat. You just can't. You can't borrow money from him.

LAYLA. Why, my darling?

ZARA. Because…

LAYLA. Zahra, what is / wrong?

HUSSEIN. Ya, woman, enough! It is too late. We agree. I already tell council.

ZARA. …What?

HUSSEIN. I make application. I sign papers – My girl, what is wrong with you?

ZARA *is swaying. She retches, then suddenly runs out of the room. The family is bewildered.*

7. Saturday lunch, just after Scene Six / Saturday evening, a few hours after Scene Three

ALICE *is sitting on the floor, slightly tipsy from champagne.* ZARA *enters to join her, from the bathroom.*

ALICE. You okay?

ZARA. Yeah.

ALICE. You just been sick?

ZARA (*vehement*). No!

ALICE. Thought I heard you...

> ZARA *shakes her head and sits beside* ALICE *on the floor.*

You still haven't told me how they took it.

ZARA. What?

ALICE. Your parents. Losing their favourite son-in-law.

ZARA. Oh... Well. They took it... well.

> *On the other side of the space, we see* HUSSEIN *gesticulating furiously, while* LAYLA *tries to calm him down.*

ALICE. See? I told you! It's *you* they care about. They love *you*. All that panic over nothing!

ZARA. Yeah, you were right.

> *That wasn't totally convincing.* ALICE *studies* ZARA.

ALICE. What's wrong?

ZARA. Nothing. I'm just a bit tipsy. Where is everyone?

ALICE. Fashionably late... Seriously, are you *okay*? You sure nothing else happened? At your dad's?

ZARA. He called me 'haram' a couple of times but nothing out of the ordinary.

ALICE. Because you would tell me, right? You can always tell me.

HUSSEIN (*to* LAYLA). Why she is behaving like this?

LAYLA. Shh. Hussein.

HUSSEIN. I don't care she hear me. It is disrespectful, Layla!

ALICE. Zara. Seriously. I'm here and you can talk to me...

HUSSEIN. Something strange is happening. I am going to call Amira.

LAYLA. Please, Hussein. ***Do not ruin dinner.***

HUSSEIN. I will be back in one minutes, woman!

He leaves. LAYLA *is exasperated.* FATIMA *is concerned.*

FATIMA. Mama, you should rest. Sit down if you –

LAYLA (*snapping*). I am fine. I will get dessert ready.

ALICE (*to* ZARA)....About anything.

FATIMA. Okay, let me help...

LAYLA. No. No, you wait for Zahra.

LAYLA *exits, leaving* FATIMA *alone. Unsure of what to do with herself,* FATIMA *picks up her iPad.*

ZARA (*to* ALICE). Nothing is wrong.

ALICE. But if it is, you can tell me. You know that right?

Beat. Will ZARA *tell her? The doorbell rings.* ALICE *leaps up, excitedly, the conversation forgotten.*

Oh shit oh shit that's them!

8. Saturday lunch, shortly after Scene Six

A few moments later. FATIMA *is studying her iPad, singing her lyrics to herself.*

FATIMA. It's not our space... it's not our place... The only place I've ever known and yet I don't –

> ZARA *enters, worse for wear. She has just been sick.* FATIMA *stops. They stare at each other.*

What?

ZARA. What?

FATIM (*wrinkling her nose*). Have you just been sick?

ZARA. No!

FATIMA (*kissing her teeth*). You're a liar, man. You're hungover and now you're throwing up.

ZARA. I'm not.

FATIMA. Drinking is bad for you, you know.

ZARA. Gee, thanks, doc. Where's Dad?

FATIMA. On the phone. Mum's making dessert.

> ZARA *makes a decision to try and connect with her sister. She peeks over her shoulder at the iPad.*

ZARA. What are you doing?

FATIMA (*moving so* ZARA *can't see*)....Revising.

ZARA. Look, I want to say... I'm sorry that I haven't been around, these last few months...

FATIMA. Bit late for *that*.

ZARA. But I'll talk to them, okay? It's not a good time to be moving you. When you've got exams and –

FATIMA. I don't care about exams. I'm not you, innit, I'm not the golden girl. I can fail A levels in Holloway and I can fail 'em in Brent. It don't matter. You can stop pretending to be worried.

ZARA. I'm not pretending. This is your future, Fatima. And this moving to Brent –

FATIMA. It ain't my future. It's exams.

ZARA. You can't just… drive cabs!

FATIMA. Why not? Baba does.

ZARA. And he hates it!

FATIMA. Whatever. Anyway it's not just driving, it's a five-year business plan. I spend three, four years with Uber, study their model from the inside, save up, then jack their best drivers to start up *my* company.

ZARA. Right. Which will be…?

FATIMA. Women's-only cabs –

ZARA. Doesn't that exist?

FATIMA. For Muslims.

ZARA. That's ridiculous.

FATIMA. No it ain't, it's genius. Spot a gap in the market and fill it. That's the first rule of business. And it's dangerous out on these streets for sisters –

ZARA. Oh come on, it's not *that* bad. It's not like we're in some war zone –

FATIMA. We *are*, bruv. That's exactly what we're in. England don't want girls like us. Even with all… this – (*Gesturing at* ZARA.) that you're carrying on with. They don't want you.

ZARA. Well of course, if you think like that…

FATIMA. I don't *think* like that. I *live* like that. And I don't wanna be scared every time a drunk white boy gets on my bus any more.

Done here, FATIMA *goes back to her iPad.* ZARA *studies her. Suddenly, with the swift, practised skill of a big sister, she grabs the iPad out of* FATIMA's *hands and playfully runs across the room.* FATIMA *leaps up.*

Give it back!

ZARA. What are you always doing on this? Messaging boys?

FATIMA. Don't be stupid! Give it –

ZARA. What's this?

FATIMA. Don't you dare fucking read that!

ZARA. Why?

FATIMA. It's private.

ZARA (*reading aloud*). 'Ask me where I'm from. Well, where do I start?' Is it a song?

FATIMA. Seriously. Give it back or you die!

FATIMA *chases* ZARA, *but* ZARA *is taller and faster. She dodges her and continues to read aloud.*

ZARA (*mock emotion*). '...Hopes they might reveal... of going back some day.'

FATIMA. Shut up!

ZARA. Gosh, Fatti! Never took you for a tortured poet! (*Mocking.*) 'England's not our home, England's not our...'

ZARA *trails off as she reads, struck.* FATIMA *gives up chasing her and sits down, sulking. When* ZARA *finishes reading, she looks at her sister.*

Fatima...

FATIMA. I told you not to read it. It's not finished.

ZARA. I didn't know you wrote like this.

FATIMA. Why would you?

ZARA. Have Mum and Dad read it?

FATIMA. No. And don't you dare show them.

ZARA (*suddenly realising*). You're... you're pretending, aren't you? You don't write like this and get 2's in English. Are you failing on purpose?

FATIMA. You breathe a word and I'll tell Baba you drink.

A beat. They stare at each other. ZARA caves first. She reads from the iPad again.

ZARA. Is this all really... what you think?

FATIMA. Yes.

ZARA. Fatima, it's not... it's not quite that black and white.

FATIMA. Nah. Iss brown.

ZARA. I didn't *choose* to change, you know. Nobody does. I had to. And you will too, one day.

FATIMA. Not me, / bruv.

ZARA. You will. This little world they've built for us... it's not England. And once you see *actual* England, you'll learn. You'll want to be part of it. Uni...

FATIMA. I ain't going uni.

ZARA. What?

FATIMA. I don't need to learn the things you did. I like who I am.

FATIMA adjusts her headscarf for emphasis. Noting this, ZARA can't stop herself.

ZARA. Please be careful, Fatima.

FATIMA. Of what?

ZARA. Choose carefully. Wearing that *will* hold you back.

FATIMA. From what? Drinking and fucking around and eating falafel / wraps?

ZARA. From *everything*. You wear that, and all people will ever see when they look at you is Mum and Dad. You'll be just like them.

FATIMA. What's wrong with that?

FATIMA waits for an answer, which ZARA cannot give. FATIMA is disgusted.

See, at least I believe in *something*. You... I would never stand at the back of the room, *pretending* to do *Salat* like Baba can't tell you ain't really praying. You lie to *everyone*.

And maybe you got them fooled: Mama, Baba, even Jamil –
but I see you. You hate us. You hate everything you are.
You'd dash us aside in a *minute* for the chance to be one
of… them. *English*. And what's sad is you ain't. You'll never
be. They don't give a shit about you –

ZARA. That's not true. Alice. Alice is my –

FATIMA (*laughing*). That posh girl you roll with? You're her
pet, man.

ZARA. Fuck off.

FATIMA. What? Am I hitting in a nerve? It's coz it's true.
She'll always make sure you're second best. That she's the
star and you're in orbit. Trust me. That's what they / do –

ZARA. You're a kid. You don't know anything.

FATIMA. Really? Coz I know Mama and Baba would give you
anything. The clothes off their back. Their *home*. And you just
throw it back in their face, every time. You make me sick.

ZARA *moves away, fed up with* FATIMA. *But* FATIMA*'s not
done yet. She calls after her.*

Mama's ill again. (*At* ZARA*'s face.*) Yeah. I saw the letters
from the hospital. Loads of them. I called you. I called and
called and called and you didn't answer. So *I* had to read
them, translate them for her. Give her the bad news. She ain't
even told Baba.

…You do you, innit. But *one* of us has to take care of her.
Ask me again why I ain't going uni.

Before ZARA *can answer,* LAYLA *enters, breaking the
tension with her busy energy.*

LAYLA. Girls! Your baba still not here?

FATIMA. He's on the phone, Mama. *Can I help?*

LAYLA. *This man!* No, I am fine. Everything is okay here?

FATIMA *speaks confidently, almost daring* ZARA *to
contradict.*

FATIMA. Great, Mama, yeah, Zara's just been helping me with revision. Do you mind if I have that back so I can check the answers?

Caught out, ZARA *hands the iPad back.*

LAYLA. Oh that is very good! Thank you, Zahra!

FATIMA. Yes, thank you, Zahra.

ZARA. It's… it's nothing.

LAYLA. You are good sisters. Let us not wait for your *akhmar* father. I make a special dessert. You want?

FATIMA. Yes! Did you make *kleicha*?

LAYLA. No. Is even more special. Zahra?

ZARA. Oooh, no thanks I'm still full.

LAYLA. You hardly eat!

ZARA. My stomach's a bit… rich food…

LAYLA (*very concerned*). You are sick?

ZARA. No, I –

FATIMA *coughs, something that sounds like 'hungover'.* ZARA *shoots her a look.*

LAYLA. You must eat yoghurt if you are sick. Good for stomach.

ZARA. I'll just have a bit of water –

LAYLA. I will bring yoghurt.

ZARA. Mum, honestly, please don't. I'm not sick.

LAYLA. Good! Then you can have my dessert! (*At* ZARA*'s protest.*) Just a little! I make special for you.

ZARA *sees the earnest hope in her mother's face and cannot say no.*

ZARA. Okay. Thank you.

As LAYLA *goes to exit,* HUSSEIN *enters. He is different, somehow heavier than the last time we saw him.*

LAYLA. *Finally!* You are hungry?

HUSSEIN *doesn't answer, he just stares at* ZARA. LAYLA *is confused.*

Okay... I will bring.

LAYLA *exits to the kitchen.* HUSSEIN *indicates to* ZARA *and* FATIMA *to sit. They comply. An awkward beat.*

FATIMA....Baba?

HUSSEIN (*shushing her*). Sssh.

LAYLA *enters, proudly carrying a large tray of home-made spotted dick, and a huge bowl of very yellow custard.*

LAYLA. Here it is!

Everyone is a bit surprised.

ZARA. Wow, Mum, that looks...

LAYLA (*very pleased*). Is a... spotty dick!

FATIMA *snorts with laughter.* LAYLA *is confused by this reaction.*

It is... English dessert. You like English food I think, Zahra?

ZARA. I... Yes, Mum, I love it. Thank you.

LAYLA. Good. Then please have, have.

LAYLA *starts serving the pudding up to them in dessert bowls. She hands one to* HUSSEIN.

HUSSEIN. Ya, what this is, Layla?

LAYLA. Cake. With a raisin. And custard – a traditional English. At least please try, Hussein.

HUSSEIN. Layla, remember when we cross the border and those government bastards beat me and all the time they laugh like this bla– like this boys in my cabs? I remember I think to myself: One day, me and my beautiful wife will reach England. She will cook her delicious food, just like back home, and we will be safe. Happy, full, and safe. This is what keep me alive. So now why you try to kill me with this disgusting / dick?

ZARA *intervenes, trying to lighten the mood.*

ZARA. Come on, Dad, it won't kill you to eat something English!

FATIMA. Why should he? Our food's the best in the world. Fact.

ZARA. You've never tried to eat anything else!

HUSSEIN. *This ice cream, Fatima. What is the name?*

FATIMA. Yeah! Magnum!

ZARA.... What?

FATIMA. We've tried Magnum ice cream. That's banging and it's *Belgian*. I bought some in Iceland yesterday. You want one?

HUSSEIN. Yes. I cannot eat *this*.

FATIMA *exits to get the ice cream.*

LAYLA. You don't like at all, Hussein?

HUSSEIN. No, Layla. It is disgusting.

ZARA. Well I think it's delicious, and it's really mean of you both to not even try –

HUSSEIN *suddenly turns on* ZARA, *cold.*

HUSSEIN. Zahra, my whole life I am force to try new things. Immigration form. Citizenship test. English weather... (*Pointed.*) Young people who respect nothing. And now I am not even safe in my own home? (*Pushing his bowl away.*) No. I will not try any more new things.

Seeing her mother upset, ZARA *is riled.*

ZARA. What about us, Dad? Don't *we* get to try new stuff? Fatima, for example?

FATIMA (*re-entering with Magnums*). What? Why you bringing me –

ZARA. Don't you want her to go uni? Coz move her now, in her last year, you jeopardise her grades...

FATIMA. Mind your business, man!

HUSSEIN. Zahra, you do not tell me how to raise / my –

ZARA. What about Mum? Perhaps she could *try* having a rest every once in a while? Rather than working until she's sick?

LAYLA *looks at* FATIMA *in panic*. FATIMA *hisses at* ZARA.

FATIMA. Shut up!

HUSSEIN. What are you talking about? Your mother is fine, so is your sister –

LAYLA (*covering*). Yes, my health is okay, Zahra.

ZARA. You don't have to say that, Mum –

HUSSEIN. I decide what is best, I am the –

LAYLA. Really I am fine –

HUSSEIN *hates losing control of the conversation and shouts* LAYLA *down*.

HUSSEIN. YA, QUIET, WOMAN! (*To* ZARA.) A daughter does not tell her father how to run his family, *khalas*. You will show me respect.

ZARA. So you can take your daughter's money, but not her advice?

A dangerous beat.

HUSSEIN.…What you say to me?

ZARA. I'm saying. I've made sacrifices for this family too –

HUSSEIN. I never ask you, Zahra…

ZARA. But you took it all the same. You must've known. Some months I barely make rent –

FATIMA. No one told you to move out. Not Baba's fault you wanna roll like some rich girl –

ZARA. Says the girl who sits on her fat arse, criticising Mum like she's some sort of slave…

HUSSEIN. Enough, *khalas*.

FATIMA. I treat her better than you!

LAYLA. Zahra please, do not worry, I am not upset about the spotty di–

ZARA. You are! Clearly you are! And Dad just –

> HUSSEIN *loses his cool and shouts. For a second it is genuinely frightening.*

HUSSEIN. I said, *KHALAS*!

> *Everyone stops, stunned by his anger. A silence.*

Zahra, where is Jamil?

…Where is Jamil?

> ZARA *can't respond.* HUSSEIN *turns to the family.*

I just speak to Amira on phone. She says there will be no wedding. I ask her why. She tell me this girl, this *foolish* girl… she ruin everything. So there is no wedding.

ZARA. I wanted to tell you…

HUSSEIN. He do something bad to you? He lay his hand on you?

ZARA. No!

HUSSEIN. Then what is the problem? Why you do this?

> ZARA *won't answer.*

Donkey girl!

LAYLA. Hussein…

HUSSEIN. *This*, Layla! This is what this country do to our children. ***This is how it starts. I warned you. Look at how she dresses.***

ZARA. My clothes?

LAYLA. The way she dresses is fine, darling.

ZARA (*almost laughing*). You think my *clothes* are the problem?

HUSSEIN. When you stop wearing hijab, Zahra?

LAYLA. Hussein, that is her business, we agree to let her –

HUSSEIN. *You* agree, not me. When you stop practising Islam, Zahra? Your little sister, she is reading Koran, coming to Mosque –

ZARA. Coz she's been brainwashed!

FATIMA. 'Scuse you?!

HUSSEIN (*angry now*). You call your religion brainwash?

ZARA (*with equal force*). Yes, I do! And you've got no right to be angry! You're the one who sent me out there, told me to get an education. Well I got educated! And maybe that means I don't want to waste my life married to some halfwit Muslim Del Boy who lives at home with his mum!

HUSSEIN. Enough.

ZARA. No! I've done what you asked of me my whole life. And all it's done is hold me back. You think you're protecting us? This place is a prison. Look at Fatima.

FATIMA. Shut the fuck up.

LAYLA. Fatima!

ZARA. Did you know she writes poems? They're beautiful. They're incredible actually and she's never going to show you because you won't understand.

HUSSEIN. Is this true, Fatima?

FATIMA. No!

ZARA (*to* FATIMA). Tell them, it's the only way.

FATIMA. It's none of your business!

ZARA. Mum, Dad – Fatima is failing on purpose.

LAYLA. On purpose?

ZARA. Yep. She's not stupid at all. In fact she's very very clever. (*To* HUSSEIN.) Cleverer than you, and me, but she's been hiding it. Because of *you*. Fatima's lying to you and you're so blind you can't see.

HUSSEIN. Fatima?

FATIMA. Zara's hungover because she got drunk last night!

Beat. HUSSEIN *looks shocked. Now he turns on* ZARA.

HUSSEIN. You drink?

ZARA....No!

FATIMA (*mocking her*). 'Tell them, Zahra, it's the only way!'

HUSSEIN. You drink alcohol?

FATIMA. And she hasn't eaten any food. She just keeps folding it into that napkin.

ZARA. What? That's not true!

FATIMA. Show us then!

ZARA. Fuck off!

LAYLA. Zahra!

HUSSEIN *grabs* ZARA*'s napkin and opens it.*

HUSSEIN. She's right, Layla, I can see all the food.

LAYLA *is genuinely hurt.*

ZARA. It's not what it...

HUSSEIN. Amira say this. I do not believe her. Jamil says Zahra will not eat.

ZARA. Jamil is an idiot. Of course I eat.

FATIMA. Eat that then.

ZARA. No!

HUSSEIN (*serious*). I would like to see you eat, Zahra.

FATIMA. Yeah, go on!

ZARA *doesn't move.*

Flipsake we ain't got all day. Here...

FATIMA *grabs a bowl and spoon and comes towards* ZARA.

LAYLA. Girls...

ZARA. Get away from me / you bi–

FATIMA. Here comes the aeroplane!

> FATIMA *waves the spoon in* ZARA*'s face.* ZARA *bats it away, angry.* FATIMA *is laughing, which makes* ZARA *angrier.*

LAYLA. Fatima, is not funny. Stop!

FATIMA. Why? You always defend her, man! Can't you see how she looks down on you? She won't even eat our food, she's that above us! Well, this is English, so go on!

> FATIMA *shoves the spoon at* ZARA*'s face.* ZARA *grabs her hands to stop her. They are getting custard everywhere.*

(*Laughing.*) YUMMMM! English food for the English girl!

> *At this,* ZARA *loses her temper. She shoves* FATIMA *hard, knocking her backwards. The bowl falls and breaks.*

> *A hiatus. Then* FATIMA *screams. She's cut her hand on the bowl, badly. Suddenly she's* ZARA*'s little sister again, fighting back tears.* LAYLA *springs to action, wrapping* FATIMA*'s hand in napkin.* HUSSEIN *turns on* ZARA.

HUSSEIN. Are you crazy? This is your sister!

ZARA. It was an accident…

LAYLA (*to* FATIMA). ***My darling, are you okay?***

HUSSEIN. Why you do this? What is wrong with you?

ZARA. I don't know, I…

> LAYLA *stands. She comes towards* ZARA, *about to say something. Terrified,* ZARA *runs.*

9. Early Saturday evening, exactly as in Scene Three

ALICE *has just spilt the dip on herself.* ZARA *appears carrying shopping bags. She looks exhausted, broken. But the second* ALICE *spots her she collects herself, hiding her feelings so proficiently it's like they were never there.*

ALICE. Thank fucking God! Baba ganoush?

ZARA. What?

ALICE. Baba ganoush! I text you asking to get the recipe from your mum!

ZARA. Oh... sorry.

ALICE. I can't cook, mine's a mess! Fix it please! And can you lay those out? I've got to change my top.

ALICE *exits, leaving* ZARA *alone.* ZARA *begins to open the packets of food on the table. But then she stops. She begins to cry, heaving racking sobs. But then she stops, gathers herself.*

Lights down.

ACT TWO

1. Saturday night

ALICE *and* ZARA*'s kitchen. A party in full swing, rubbish everywhere. Music plays offstage, that nostalgic stage of the night where people are playing the songs they danced to as teenagers.* ANTHONY *enters. Mid-thirties, handsome, comfortable in his skin. He's wearing a suit. He looks around for someone, then notices the table, covered in a cloth. He tiptoes over, lifts up the tablecloth.* ZARA *is there, chomping on Pringles. She nearly jumps out of her skin, spits out the crisps.*

ZARA. Anthony! (*To herself, quiet.*) *Such a fucking pig!*

ANTHONY. Sorry?

ZARA. Nothing.

ANTHONY. Can I have some?

> ZARA *clambers out from under the table and passes the bowl to* ANTHONY, *he grabs a handful.*

> Once you pop…

> *He offers the bowl back.*

ZARA. No thanks.

ANTHONY (*chomping*). You okay?

ZARA. Yeah. Why?

ANTHONY. You were under a table? Say no more, I feel you.
Your friends seem nice but it's a bit intense in / there –

ZARA. Oh, they're not my friends.

ANTHONY. Really? Alice said it was your crew from uni.

ZARA. *Her* crew, she's just being nice and sharing them.

ANTHONY. Yeah, she's a little… forceful with the sharing? (*At* ZARA*'s face*.) the strained small talk, the being dragged round the room, the reeling off your credentials…

ZARA. Welcome to life with Alice Reilly.

ANTHONY. Phew. I'm gonna need more crisps! (*Grabs another handful, studies* ZARA.) How's your day been?

ZARA. Good, thanks.

ANTHONY. You're allowed to answer properly.

ZARA. How's *yours* been?

ANTHONY. Not the best. Man in my corner shop accused me of stealing today. Called me some pretty rough names.

ZARA (*genuinely shocked*). Does that still happen to you?

ANTHONY. Yep. Even with the suit.

ZARA. That's shit.

ANTHONY. Yep. Your turn.

He smiles at her, genuine. ZARA *would love to talk to someone. But it's difficult.*

ZARA. My day was… (*Diverting.*) Phew! I'm drunk. And I really didn't want to be.

ANTHONY. Anything I can do?

ZARA. Make me a drink?

ANTHONY. Okay. Water or…?

ZARA. A. Drink.

ANTHONY. You sure?

ZARA. *Yes.* I want to drown my sorrows. And I've finished the wine no one else would touch.

ANTHONY. Lidl! Sound choice. I'll knock up something special.

ANTHONY *goes to make a drink.* ZARA *takes a seat, studying him intently. He turns back to say something and catches her. She's embarrassed and looks away.*

ZARA. – You're not wearing a costume.

ANTHONY. I came from work. What's your excuse?

ZARA. I'm Muslim. I can't wear slutty clothes without hearing my forefathers shouting: 'SHAME!'

ANTHONY. Mate, I know. But you're lucky. If *my* forefathers saw me necking Lidl's finest I wouldn't live to see tomorrow – what?

ZARA. You're Muslim?

ANTHONY. Not really. My father is. (*Amused.*) What?

ZARA. I thought you were Jamaican!

ANTHONY. Why did you think that?

ZARA. Alice is always saying how you make amazing jerk chicken. Made her break her veganism.

ANTHONY. I *do* make amazing jerk chicken. And Thai green curry, and shepherd's pie. Also there is such a thing as a Jamaican Muslim.

ZARA. But are you –

ANTHONY. Brummie? Yeah.

ZARA. No, where are you...

ANTHONY (*laughing*). Aw hell NO, you are NOT about to ask me where I'm *really* from!

ZARA. I didn't mean, I was just... curious...

ANTHONY. Shame on you, girl!

After everything that's happened today, ZARA*'s extra-sensitive. She doesn't realise* ANTHONY *is joking.*

ZARA (*desperate outburst*). I'm sorry! I'm really sorry. I'm stupid, I'm an idiot, I shouldn't have asked.

An awkward beat. ANTHONY *eases the tension.*

ANTHONY....Zara? I'm teasing! My folks were born in Nigeria, but I've never been. (*Teasing her.*) Listen, don't sweat it. I thought you were Syrian till about an hour ago.

But then I heard you school that girl in there – Annabel? Boy! Glad it weren't me!

ZARA. Fucking Annabel. I've known her nearly ten years, and she still can't remember where I'm from. At our last party she told people the reason I can't drive is coz I'm Saudi.

ANTHONY. She asked me if I'd come as Barack Obama.

ZARA. Obama?

ANTHONY. I said 'Nah, bab, this is a *white*-trash party. I'm Donald Trump!'

They share a smile.

ZARA. I'm sorry I thought you were Jamaican.

ANTHONY. Don't sweat it. I'm sorry I thought you were Syrian.

I don't get the whole costume thing, do you? How am I supposed to dress as 'white trash'? Ain't that cultural appropriation?

ZARA. Only if we 'white up'…

ANTHONY. Well, there *is* that tub of sour cream over there…

ZARA belly-laughs despite herself.

Whew, so she does laugh.

ZARA. I'm sorry, I'm not normally… I guess you *could* say I've had a bad day too.

ANTHONY approaches with two drinks, hands one to ZARA.

ANTHONY. Yeah, I heard you broke up with your man or something? And that it's complicated because it was… arranged? (*At* ZARA*'s face.*) Sorry, you don't have to talk about it…

ZARA. Arranged? Who told you that?

ANTHONY. Aw, my bad, must've got the wrong end / of the –

ZARA. He was my boyfriend from school. Did Alice say it was arranged?

ANTHONY. I probably... misunderstood. So what was it? Was he just a dickhead? Standard stuff?

ZARA. He bought us a flat.

ANTHONY. Oh... Right. So you're getting back together?

ZARA. No. But that's what my family want.

ANTHONY. Do you want him back?

ZARA. I don't think he'd have me.

ANTHONY. But do *you* want him?

ZARA. ...No.

> *As* ZARA *says this,* ANTHONY *and her lock eyes, probably for the first time. They suddenly become very aware they're alone together.* ZARA *breaks the tension, tasting her drink.*

> This is amazing!

ANTHONY. When we met... you said pomegranate is your favourite fruit, so I added a dash of that, some lime, bit of rum – I've not made it strong...

ZARA. You've got a good memory. It's delicious.

ANTHONY (*genuinely pleased*). Thanks.

ZARA. What have *you* got?

ANTHONY. Ah, just a Coke. (*Off her face.*) Don't drink.

ZARA. Oh. Coz of... Allah?

ANTHONY (*amused*). Coz I didn't want to any more?

ZARA. What do you do at parties?

ANTHONY. What do you mean?

ZARA. *I* didn't used to drink, thought it was haram. But when I went to university there wasn't any other way to socialise.

ANTHONY. You didn't try to talking to people?

ZARA. About what? The hundreds of things we have in common? Easier to get pissed.

ANTHONY. Yeah, getting laggered *was* about eighty per cent of my friendships. But I definitely found out who my real mates were when I stopped – What?

ZARA. Nothing. Just, Alice never mentioned that. About you. (*Sudden realisation.*) Oh gosh, I forgot! Cheers! To your new love nest!

ANTHONY. Love nest? Don't you mean all three of us? (*Realising how it sounds.*) As flatmates, obviously...

ZARA *just turns away, drinks.*

What? Have I put my foot in it?

ZARA. No, no...

ANTHONY. Promise I'll put the toilet seat down. And I'm very clean.

ZARA. It's not that.

ANTHONY. I can probably find a way of making vegan jerk chicken –

ZARA. No I just, I don't wanna get in your way, it would be crowded...

ANTHONY. Crowded? This is London mate! I used to live in a one-bed with four lads, we took shifts sleeping in the bathtub –

ZARA. I'd be a third wheel.

ANTHONY. No you won't! And you know, if you're looking to date, I can introduce you to my / mates!

ZARA. Anthony – I can't really stay.

ANTHONY. Why?

A beat. ZARA *sighs, turns to him.*

ZARA. Coz... I know Alice. She's desperate to start a life with someone, with *you*. She's too nice to tell me, but I'll get in the way. I've already done that enough.

ANTHONY. This is your home though.

ZARA. She's been doing me a favour here. It was never gonna last forever.

ALICE (*offstage*). ZARA?

ZARA. Fuck.

ZARA *leaps up and crawls under the table.*

ANTHONY. What are you doing?

ZARA. Shush! Please, she wants me to talk to Michael and I promised and she'll be cross…

ANTHONY. What do you expect me to / say?

ZARA. Tell her I've gone out.

ALICE (*offstage*). Zara!

ZARA *pulls the tablecloth down to cover herself.*
ANTHONY *jumps up as* ALICE *enters. He can't help looking shifty.*

ANTHONY. Alright?

ALICE. Oh hi, there you are. You seen Zara?

ANTHONY. I think she… stepped out.

ALICE. *Really?* Argh! What's wrong with her tonight? She's been miserable all evening. I tried to get her to talk to Michael, he's practically *salivating* over her, and she just goes silent and wanders off. She was going to get him a drink about an hour ago.

ANTHONY. Maybe she just… doesn't want to be salivated over.

ALICE. He's *gagging* to offer her a job, Anthony! A much better / one!

ANTHONY. Shall we head back in?

ALICE *sighs, flops onto a stool and reaches out her hand.*

ALICE. Not yet, please. Sit with me?

ANTHONY *struggles for a moment, looking at the table* ZARA *is hiding under.*

ANTHONY.…Course.

He goes over to ALICE, *puts his hands on her back.*
Realising how tense she is, he begins to massage her.

ALICE. Ah. You're an angel.

ANTHONY. And *you're* mad tense.

ALICE. Yeah…

He gets a knot.

…nnggg… I'm really worried about this promotion.

ANTHONY. You're gonna be brilliant.

ALICE. *No.* About having to be Zara's… (*Whispers this.*) *boss*?
Things aren't going well at the office, babe. People talk
about her. She's inept. Makes mistakes on menial tasks,
forgets clients' names, I mean it's mortifying. *I* got her in
you know, and her job is *easy* –

ANTHONY (*aware* ZARA *can hear*). Bab, shall we head back
to the –

ALICE. She should be able to do it with her eyes closed. I don't
get it. We had a plan. We were *both* going to soar. And then
one day it's like… she gives up. Quits her LPC, settles for
paralegal, and then just sort of… sits there. And you know
the really fucked-up thing? Nobody's *saying* anything to her,
because…

She searches ANTHONY*'s face, deciding how to say this.*

Well because she's brown. (*Quick.*) I mean like, they're
lacking in 'diversity' so they're just letting it slide. Isn't that
so UNFAIR? On her? That nobody's sat her down and told
her what she's doing wrong, how to improve, given her
a chance to fix it?

ANTHONY (*painfully aware of* ZARA). Listen, Alice…

ALICE. So it's going to fall on me. If I'm a good mate and
a good boss I'm going to have to tell her!

…Oh God, do you think I'm horrible? Do you think I'm an
awful person for saying that?

ANTHONY. You're not awful.

ALICE. Maybe something's wrong? Because more and more these days, it's like she's not… I mean the guys tonight, they're our oldest mates and –

ANTHONY. Are you sure?

ALICE. What do you mean?

ANTHONY (*gently*). Do you *realise* how white that room is, hun?

ALICE. That's not –

ANTHONY *waits as* ALICE *realises*.

Oh. But surely that doesn't… Not when it's her friends?

ANTHONY. I *always* notice when I'm the only black person in the room. And it makes me feel… outside.

A silence while ALICE *processes that.*

Look, let's go back to the party. (*So* ZARA *can hear.*) I'M SURE ZARA WILL JOIN US / EVENTUALLY…

ALICE. No… wait. I don't think that's… fair.

ANTHONY. What isn't?

ALICE. To act like everyone in there is some… homogenous *mass* to her, just coz we've got a similar skin tone – not that I'd deny *your* experience, babe, not ever! But Zara knows these people. They're her friends. And I don't buy it. It's too… easy.

ANTHONY. Easy?

ALICE. I mean… simplistic, to blame it on … (*Hesitates, then whispers.*) race?

ANTHONY (*half-amused, half-annoyed*). You can say it, bab. It's not a swear word.

ALICE *hesitates*.

No go on, say what you're thinking, I want to know.

ALICE *eyes* ANTHONY *warily, wondering if this is dangerous territory. She begins speaking, at first hesitant but then growing more confident.*

ALICE. I don't think – and I'm only saying this as her best friend – it's anything to do with race. I'm not saying her family isn't… that the cultural stuff isn't… *complicated*… but they've made sure she had opportunities – they *adore* her! They were *all* at her graduation, cheering her on. *My* parents didn't even show! So I don't, and maybe I'm wrong, but I don't think she's struggling because of a *cultural* disadvantage.

ANTHONY. What is it then?

ALICE. I think maybe she's…

ALICE hesitates. She's never said this aloud.

I think she's lazy. Thinks the world owes her something.

ANTHONY.…Wow.

ALICE. I'm not saying that makes her – Please don't look at me like that.

ANTHONY. I just – I thought you were friends.

ALICE. We *are*. But I've been… Anthony, I've been propping her up, for nearly ten years now and it's… it just gets a bit tiring. Trying to help someone who won't help herself.

ANTHONY. Right.

An awkward pause. Something has shifted in the air. ALICE tries to change the mood.

ALICE. I'm gonna go back to everyone. Do you want to join or…

ANTHONY. Maybe in a minute.

ALICE. Fuck.

ANTHONY. What?

ALICE. I've broken something, haven't I? I didn't / mean it like –

ANTHONY. No. *No*, stop worrying. We trust each other. We're talking about difficult stuff. That's a good thing.

ALICE. Yes! Yes, exactly. (*Beaming at him.*) God, you're so… brilliant. Can't wait till you move in.

ALICE *kisses* ANTHONY, *tender and obviously mad about him. He's a little uncomfortable. She pulls away, smiling.*

Join us? When you're ready, of course. (*With a grin.*) I'll introduce you to all the whiteys!

ANTHONY (*smiling*). I'll be right behind you.

ALICE *exits, looking back at* ANTHONY. *After a moment,* ANTHONY *goes to the table and lifts the cloth.* ZARA *emerges.*

Did you...?

ZARA. Every word.

ANTHONY. Bloody hell. I'm really sorry. Are you okay?

ZARA *doesn't answer. She goes to the drinks table and pours herself another drink. She is shaking. She has her back to* ANTHONY. *Meanwhile, on the other side of the space,* FATIMA *sneaks into the living room, wearing her pyjamas. Her hand now has a dressing on it. Satisfied she won't be interrupted, she begins to work through a verse of her song as* ZARA *speaks.*

ZARA. You know, the day I started university, my dad took the whole day off work. It wasn't like he could afford it. But nothing like that had ever happened to us. My whole family drove up in his cab to York. I remember sticking my head out of the window and Baba warning me my hijab would blow off. I'd never been out of London. I'd never even had my own bedroom. And when they left me in that dorm room I spent the next three months totally alone.

...*Totally* alone. Nobody knew what to do with me, the awkward Muslim girl. So they did the easiest thing. Made me invisible. For months...

Only one person, only one, *eventually* saw me. Alice. She took me in. Showed me how it worked, how to act, all those... *codes* you don't get to learn when you're born... outside. And I worked *hard* to learn it all. Really hard. I gave up everything I was. Little Hijabi Zahra, gone. Everything. So much so that now, I look at my father and I see... (*This hurts.*) I see a

stranger I'm embarrassed by. My mother, I see… someone
I wish I wasn't related to. And I can't unsee it…

ANTHONY. Hey –

ZARA. But it was worth it I thought, because at the very, very
least I've got one person who *really sees* me. I didn't have to
pretend with Alice. I wasn't invisible.

What a fucking joke. You're always alone. Always.

ZARA *tries to hold herself together, but it's a struggle. She
breaks.* ANTHONY *can't take it. He comes over and takes
hold of her. She buries herself in his arms.*

ANTHONY. Hey. Sh. Sh. It's okay. You're not alone.

ZARA. I am.

ANTHONY. You're not.

ZARA *looks up at* ANTHONY. *And then she kisses him.
Forcefully, with passion.* ANTHONY *is surprised and
responds. For a brief moment there's electricity, danger. But
then he pulls away abruptly.*

That's not… a good idea.

ZARA. Why?

ANTHONY. Look, you're upset. You'll regret it.

ZARA. I won't.

ANTHONY. I care about Alice, Zara.

ZARA. But does she care about *you*?

ANTHONY. Excuse me?

ZARA. The things she says about you! (*Doing an impression of*
ALICE.) 'He's not the… erudite successful genius I pictured
myself with. But he's gorgeous. And sexy. And he actually
makes me cum…'

ANTHONY. Zara…

ZARA. 'Okay, I know this sounds awful, but what they say
about black men? It's ALL TRUE!'

ANTHONY. Right, stop it.

ZARA. What? It's the truth. It's what she thinks of you. I would know, she tells me *all the time*...

ANTHONY. Look, I'm not getting caught up / in some sort of...

ZARA. But don't you see? You're her *pet*. Just like me.

A silence. This comment makes ANTHONY *deeply angry. He is about to say something. But then takes a deep breath, shakes his head and moves away from* ZARA, *towards the door.*

Wait, what / are you...?

ANTHONY. This is fucked / up.

ZARA (*desperate*). *I'm* not the one who thinks those things, it's Alice –

This pisses ANTHONY *off, big time.*

ANTHONY. So why are you repeating it?!

ZARA *steps back, surprised.*

I've had to listen to that sort of shit my whole life, Zara. On a daily basis. Think I need to hear it again?

ZARA. I just thought you should know the truth...

ANTHONY. *Why?* Is it gonna make me feel better? Or does it just do *you* good, spouting that poison?

ZARA. I'm sorry, / wait –

ANTHONY *pauses at the door.*

ANTHONY. I know who I am. I'm proud of working that out. But you, you got self-hate running all through you. And trust me, that's the worst poison there is.

ANTHONY *exits. Struck by what she's done,* ZARA *stands there, alone.* FATIMA *sings, working out lyrics.*

FATIMA....Choose a mask
Be let in, shed your skin
Your truth, your faith, your past
Be let in – shed your skin –

2. Sunday, early hours

LAYLA *comes downstairs, in her pyjamas. She listens to*
FATIMA *for a moment.* FATIMA *turns and sees her, stops.*
LAYLA *speaks a mix of Arabic and English.*

LAYLA. **Carry on. Don't stop.**

FATIMA (*suddenly shy*). I can't… not in front of you…

> LAYLA *comes over to* FATIMA. *She takes hold of her hand.*

LAYLA. **Let me see. Does it hurt?**

FATIMA. A bit.

LAYLA. Fatima, your sister is not well. **We will have to help**
her. Do you understand?

> FATIMA *nods.*

> **You're a good daughter.** I love you very much. Go to bed
> okay? It is late.

FATIMA. *Aiwa*, Mama.

> FATIMA *begins to go.* LAYLA *calls after her, holding up*
> FATIMA*'s iPad.*

LAYLA. Can I borrow? I will not read anything private.
Wallahi. I promise.

FATIMA.…Okay.

> FATIMA *goes.* LAYLA *begins researching something on the*
> *iPad. She frowns. Throughout the following scene,* LAYLA
> *reads, her reactions sometimes chiming with* ZARA *and*
> ALICE*'s.*

> *Meanwhile, in* ZARA*'s flat,* ALICE *enters and flops into*
> *a seat. She is shell-shocked.* ZARA *stands beside her. The*
> *party is over and there is rubbish everywhere.* ALICE *is still*
> *in her 'white trash' outfit.*

ALICE.…I don't get it. I just don't get it.

ZARA. I'm… / sorry.

ALICE. A text. A fucking text? Everything's going great, and suddenly he's pulling the brakes – like this? (*Reading from phone*.) 'I'm sorry. I don't want to hurt you. I just don't think this is going to work.' What the fuck? Is it a joke?

> ALICE *looks at* ZARA, *surprised she hasn't jumped in*.

Zara? You're supposed to reassure me?

ZARA. Maybe… he had a good reason?

ALICE. What?!

ZARA. I mean, there's plenty of fish in the –

ALICE. It's him I want.

ZARA. *Really?*

ALICE. YES.

> ALICE *studies* ZARA, *a new thought coming to mind*.

…Where did you go earlier?

ZARA.…For air.

ALICE. That's a lot of / air.

ZARA. I'm sorry about the party.

ALICE. Yeah, you weren't the greatest host. Michael was looking for you for ages, trying to give you his card… Is everything okay?

ZARA (*cold*). Course.

ALICE. How does someone just… *drop* a person? So brutally? I've never been dumped before. God I don't wish it on anyone. Do you think Jamil feels like / this?

ZARA. Right. This calls for ice cream. I'll crack out the Ben & Jerry's.

ALICE. No.

ZARA. It's the vegan one.

ALICE. I don't want to be fat as well as single.

ZARA. You're not fat. And ice cream is like booze, it doesn't / count.

ALICE. Fine. (*As* ZARA *goes to fetch it*.) But only if you actually have some. Don't do the whole 'Oh this is delicious' thing and then only eat like one spoon while I finish the tub.

ZARA. Please. This is me you're talking to. On Wednesday I scoffed a tub in one sitting.

ALICE. Then where are you putting it? You're so skinny. (*Sudden thought*.) Did Anthony dump me coz I gained half a stone?

ZARA. Don't be / stupid –

ALICE. All podgy in a crop top... and then he sees *you*.

ZARA *offers* ALICE *a tub of ice cream and a spoon*.

Where's *your* spoon? (*Shoves it away*.) No, I don't want this. What happened last night?

ZARA. Nothing.

ALICE. So why are you looking at me like I've just said I want to make Britain great again?

ZARA. I'm not.

ALICE. Were you in here together?

ZARA. I told you, I went for a / walk.

ALICE. But you were *both* gone – for ages. Did you say something to him? Scare him off?

ZARA. No!

ALICE. Even by accident? It's just... I get the impression you don't want him to move in... (*Trying to be delicate*.) Is it like... a cultural thing? Like you can't be Muslim and live with a guy you're not...?

ZARA *laughs at* ALICE, *incredulous*. ALICE *is frustrated*.

What then? You don't like him?

ZARA. It's not me that doesn't *like* him, Alice.

ALICE. What? What's that supposed to mean?

ZARA. It's what you do, isn't it? Find cultures you don't know, exotic, exciting. And then you set about improving us, moulding us into the person *you* think we should be…

ALICE. Excuse me? Are you serious? After everything I've done, I *do* for you? That's what you think?

ZARA shrugs, moves away, but ALICE *follows, getting in* ZARA*'s path so* ZARA *has to confront her.*

You DID say something, didn't you? Oh my GOD! You cannot BEAR to see me happy, can you? Anthony, my work, you've just *got* to shit on it. You know I can see you, right? How bitter you are? Your face when I got this partnership, like a dark cloud des–

ZARA. Forgive me for struggling to stomach yet *another* Alice Reilly victory!

ALICE. I've shared everything. And I am always happy for *you*. No matter / what!

ZARA. Coz it's easy to be happy for someone who's always a step behind!

ALICE. And whose fault is that?

ZARA. I don't know, Alice! Probably a bit mine, but probably not all! All I know is good things just fall into your lap, and they don't in mine! You eat your Michelin-star meal, hand me the scraps, and act like I'm being a bitch when I dare to want a bit / more.

ALICE. I work fucking hard.

ZARA. Harder than everyone else?

ALICE. Harder than some.

ZARA. Me?

ALICE. I give it my all and I don't give up when things get difficult.

ZARA. Coz you've got trust funds and real estate to fall back on when things 'get difficult'!

ALICE (*outraged*). I pay for myself!

ZARA. Really?

ALICE. Yes!

ZARA. Ha! Let's have a look then.

> ZARA *stomps over to* ALICE*'s cupboard and throws it open. It's filled with Whole Foods Market bags and products.*

Yours.

> ZARA *opens her cupboard. Half a loaf of bread, an apple and a can of soup.*

Mine.

ALICE. What does that prove except that you don't / eat?!

ZARA (*going through* ALICE*'s cupboard*). Thought you were 'a bit broke' this month? From the family holiday in Tuscany? So who footed *this* bill? Coconut oil, matcha powder, cashew butter – gluten-free brownies?! For the last time, you are not wheat intolerant!!!

ALICE. Fuck off, it bloats / me.

ZARA. Cacao nibs, organic muesli, coconut water, I can't even pronounce / *that* –

> *She throws the offending product at* ALICE, *continues to rummage.*

ALICE. It's none of your business what I spend money / on!

ZARA. You're right, you're right. I mean, this is important isn't it? You need the right accessories! Got to be organic, vegan, fair-trade, gotta be bezzie mates with a Muslim and shacking up with a black man to prove how *woke* you are! Who knows? Get enough 'brownie' points and you might even be allowed to do the accent!

ALICE. What? You started that / joke!

ZARA. Maybe if Anthony marries you, you'll be allowed to say the N-word!

ALICE. How *dare* you?

ZARA. And if you wear enough jazzy prints, learn to make rice
and peas and baba ganoush, you might even get to shed the
awful burden of being… ooh, now that's a good title: 'White
Privilege – the Englishwoman's Burden – by Alice / Reilly'.

ALICE. Well done, Zara. But my father is Irish –

ZARA. Oh no! Oh oops! My bad. That's completely / different!

ALICE. And since when are you and Anthony the same? Your
family are *racist*, you told me! Sorry to break it to you, but
you're closer to me than him!

ZARA (*incredulous*). You think we're the same? You and me?

ALICE. Pretty much.

ZARA. Ha! Wow. Okay. Little experiment!

ZARA *grabs some fruit from* ALICE*'s cupboard. Something
exotic in nice packaging. Something that splatters. She then
pulls out the old apple from her cupboard. She holds them up.*

You and me. Both fruit right? I mean according to you. Both
got an equal chance of making it into the salad. But see…
(*The posh fruit.*) This is you. Packaged, seedless, hairless,
perfectly ripe… you're superior, you're 'Taste the
Difference' –

ALICE. Oh shut / up –

ZARA. And me, well… (*Holding up the apple.*) here I am.
Bit bruised. Bit battered. See *I* don't get an organic-food
allowance. No 'don't worry darling, we'll support you to do
as many qualifications as you want', no champagne gifts
from Daddy. I get parents who need me to bail *them* out.
I get to give up on my dreams because I can't afford to do
both. I get the *weight* of their expectations, pressing,
pushing… (*In frustration.*) ARGH! See, Alice? MY life is
more like…

ZARA *hurls the apple against a wall near* ALICE.
ALICE *ducks as it thuds to the floor.*

That. See? And look, I might end up a bit… dented, might
roll around pathetically, but I'm *okay*. I'm used to it.

(*Picking up the posh fruit*.) The thing with you is… well we don't know. You're all *smug* in this packaging. Nobody's ever chucked *you* on the floor. We don't actually know what would happen. (*Rips the wrappers off*.) Shall we find out?

ALICE. Zara, you're being / mental.

ZARA. But I want to know, don't you? Coz isn't that what you think? That I'm pathetic? You think I just 'gave up'. Out of choice. Out of laziness, when you have no idea –

ALICE. When have I ever –

ZARA. I fucking *heard* you. Earlier. I heard what you said.

ALICE *reels*.

ALICE. Zara, I didn't mean it like –

ZARA. So let's find out, shall we? What happens if you experience even *half* the shit I've had to?

At that, ZARA *hurls the exotic fruit, as hard as she can.* ALICE *cries out. It hurtles through the air and hits the wall near* ALICE, *bursting and splattering them both. Silence.* ZARA's *anger is suddenly spent.*

Shit. Sorry.

…Shit. I'll clean that up.

ALICE. Fuck you.

ZARA *gets the giggles.*

ZARA. Sorry, I didn't expect it to… oh my God, your face.

ALICE. You *were* in here, weren't you?

At ALICE's *furious face,* ZARA *starts to lose her grip, laughter becoming hysterical.*

Don't laugh! You were in here with him earlier tonight!

ZARA. I, oh God… Sorry, sorry…

ALICE. Fuck you, Zara.

ZARA *tries to pull herself together, but she just laughs harder. Enraged,* ALICE *picks up the squashed fruit, hurls it at her.*

Fuck YOUUUUUUUUUU!

The fruit misses and ZARA *just laughs harder.* ALICE *is livid. She throws herself at* ZARA, *grabbing bits of fruit and squashing it into her face. They launch into a full-on food war. It could almost be funny if they weren't so angry. Eventually, they reach a stand-off.* ZARA *has thrown everything except the jar of cashew butter she's holding. She can't bring herself to throw something that heavy at* ALICE. *She puts the jar on the counter.* ALICE's *head is bowed. Suddenly her shoulders begin to shake.* ZARA *is not sure if she is crying or laughing.*

ZARA. Alice?

ZARA instinctively goes to hold her, but ALICE *pushes her away. She is shaking with rage.* ZARA *is frightened.*

ALICE. Don't TOUCH me! What happened earlier? What did you *do*?

ZARA. Nothing.

ALICE. You're a liar.

ZARA. We… talked.

ALICE. About?

ZARA. I was very drunk, Alice.

ALICE. Oh don't pull that one. Don't insult me with that one.

ZARA. I… I was upset.

ALICE. What about?

What. About?

ZARA. You. Family. Being alone.

ALICE. Right.

ALICE *stares at* ZARA, *cold. She is not going to let her off the hook.*

ZARA. He was just… here, and I… I told him all this stuff. Stuff I've not ever… and there was a moment.

ALICE. A moment of what? (*At* ZARA*'s silence*.) A moment of WHAT?

ZARA. …I kissed him.

A beat. ALICE *is stunned. She was not expecting THAT.*

ALICE. Why?

A pause.

…Why?

ZARA. I… don't know.

ALICE. Yes you do!

ZARA. I was… angry at you. At the things you said. And I wanted… just for a moment, to –

ALICE. To hurt me? Even though I'm your fucking *friend*?

What is wrong with you? Seriously? Why are you breaking everything for no reason?

ZARA. That's not –

ALICE. Isn't it? I mean was what I said *that* untrue, Zara?

ZARA. You have no idea –

ALICE. Coz you won't tell me! Is it because you don't eat?

ZARA freezes. Meanwhile, LAYLA *reads something that shocks her, gasps. She stands, moves to the window to think.*

I'm not stupid. I keep finding chewed-up food in napkins. The toilet smells like vomit. What is happening to you?

Talk to me. I'm supposed to be your friend and I don't fucking understand you.

ZARA. …I can't.

ALICE. Why did you kiss my boyfriend?

ZARA. I don't know.

ALICE. Well fucking try to know.

ZARA. For a brief moment I thought we understood each other. I thought… he was mine.

ALICE. And I just didn't feature. In that moment?

ZARA. …No.

ALICE. I don't know who you are.

> *Pause.* ALICE *takes a deep breath. She finds it very painful to say this.*

I don't think we can live together any more. I *want* us to be bigger than a bloke. I want you to be the sister I chose. But I have no idea what's going on in your / head –

ZARA. I'm sorry, please –

ALICE. Too late… Fuck!

ZARA. What?

ALICE. I need a hug. I need a hug and it can't be you any more.

> ALICE *begins to cry.* ZARA *stands there, helpless. Desperate to comfort her, but knowing it is too late.*

3. Sunday morning

ALICE *heads to her room. After a beat,* ZARA *exits to her own room, crushed. In the family home,* LAYLA *remains standing by the window. She has been up most of the night reading.* HUSSEIN *enters from the kitchen, munching on leftover spotted dick.* LAYLA *turns, catching him. They speak a mix of Arabic and English.*

LAYLA. So now you like?

HUSSEIN. There is nothing else to eat!

LAYLA (*playful*). **Liar.**

> *Caught out,* HUSSEIN *is apologetic. Remorseful about his behaviour the day before.*

HUSSEIN. *I am sorry, Layla.* Your husband very stupid. I am sorry.

LAYLA. *You speak to Jamil?*

HUSSEIN. This *kelb* son-in-law does not answer me.

> HUSSEIN *is heavier than we've ever seen him.* LAYLA
> *takes his hand.*

LAYLA. We will find a way. *Alhamdulillah,* we are tough family.

HUSSEIN. Yes. (*Kisses her.*) *I love you.*

LAYLA. *I love you too.* Do not work too hard. Be safe.

HUSSEIN. *Inshallah.*

LAYLA. And no more eating these… what is name…
CUSTARD CREAMS! I want healthy husband, living till he
is one hundred!

> HUSSEIN *laughs, nods and leaves. Alone,* LAYLA *makes
> a decision. She goes to the dresser and retrieves an old
> address book, rifles for a number and dials. Someone
> answers.* LAYLA *stumbles slightly.*

Hello? Hello, sorry I call you too early, this is Layla Al-Attas,
Zahra's mother?

> LAYLA *talks quietly on the phone. We can't hear her. In the
> flat we see* ZARA *enter. She hasn't slept and looks terrible.*
> LAYLA *hangs up the phone. Meanwhile,* ALICE *enters from
> outside, still wearing her party clothes, but also a jacket and
> hat.* ZARA *stands eagerly.* ALICE *faces her. A beat:*

ZARA.…Morning.

ALICE. Morning.

ZARA. I… I heard you leave. Where did you go?

ALICE. Walk. It's nice out.

> *Silence.*

ZARA. Coffee?

ALICE. No thanks.

> *Silence.*

ZARA. I…

ALICE. I woke up and I'd forgot what happened. Nearly came to your room and climbed in the bed.

ZARA. You'd have been / welcome…

ALICE. No. I went to see Anthony instead.

ZARA freezes.

It was good actually. At least honest. At least I can say it was that.

ZARA. Alice –

ALICE. He had a lot to say.

ZARA. Alice, it's my fault. I said terrible stuff to him…

ALICE. I know. He told me. But they were things *I* said.

ZARA. I only did it to hurt him like I was hurting. He should be angry at *me*, not you. (*Hesitant.*) If you want I'll call him to / explain –

ALICE. No.

ZARA. Alice, I'm so so – [sorry].

ALICE. 'The Unwitting Supremacist'. (*At* ZARA*'s face.*) Title of my biog– You're right, it's awful.

Beat. ALICE *tries to explain, struggling to find the words.*

See I've got this memory… it still makes my skin… *crawl*… of telling this girl I was prettier than her, I was the princess, fair skin, straight hair. I don't know where I learnt that. I was four. I remember her face, how hurt and angry she was, I… so I made a pact. To never be that girl again. But then… Every now and again…

…Does it upset you when I joke about your family? When I do the voice?

ZARA. …Sometimes.

ALICE (*processing this*). Okay.

ZARA (*light*). But I started the joke, and we're sisters, so you get special privileges –

ALICE. *No*. No, I *don't* get that privilege. You have a sister, Zara. I'm your – I *was* your friend.

Pause. ZARA *processes the weight of that. Nods.*

ZARA. Right. Okay. I'll start looking for places. This afternoon.

ALICE. Yeah, that's probably best.

A painful pause. This hurts them both. ZARA *suddenly blurts out, desperately.*

ZARA. Alice, I'll make it up to you, / please...

ALICE. No. Things are... different. We've both got some thinking to –

ZARA. I'll behave better, I'll be a better friend.

ALICE. It's not about you *behaving better*, Zara!

The doorbell rings. ALICE *clocks it. She turns to* ZARA.

It's about *getting* better. You should get that.

ZARA*'s confused, but she goes to the door. Unable to stop herself,* ALICE *blurts out:*

ALICE. Don't fuck him. Don't ever fuck him.

ZARA. I... No. I won't.

ALICE *nods, gestures to the door.* ZARA *opens it and finds* LAYLA *standing there. She is stunned.*

LAYLA. Hello, Zahra. Hello, Aliis.

ALICE. Morning, Mrs Al-Attas. I'll just... I'll leave you guys to it.

ALICE *leaves, self-conscious about her outfit in* LAYLA*'s presence.* ZARA *and* LAYLA *are left alone. Awkward silence.*

LAYLA. Zahra?

ZARA. You should've warned me you were coming...

LAYLA. You will tell me no. Can I come in?

ZARA doesn't move, so LAYLA *steps round* ZARA *and into the flat.* ZARA *sees her mum take in the sticky floor, the mess from the food fight and the party. She is mortified.*

ZARA. The place is a mess… Alice had a party –

LAYLA. Is fine. Is nice.

To prove her point, LAYLA *moves some clothes off a surface and sits.*

(*Pointed.*) …And not too far from us. One train. It take me thirty minutes.

ZARA. Oh. Right… Yes. When it's not… rush hour, it can be quite quick.

LAYLA *looks at her, not buying it for a second.* ZARA *is desperately uncomfortable.*

Um… Do you want some tea?

LAYLA. Please.

ZARA. How do you take it?

That's not really a question LAYLA *ever gets asked.*

You know, milk, sugar?

LAYLA. I will… have like you have.

ZARA. Okay. (*Checking fridge.*) Shit. I mean, Oh no.

LAYLA. What?

ZARA. Alice only has cashew milk. And agave nectar.

LAYLA. Okay.

ZARA. You might not like it…

LAYLA. I will try.

ZARA *begins to make tea.* LAYLA *studies her.*

Your friend Aliis. She change so much. Use to be very skinny.

ZARA. Mum!

LAYLA. What?

ZARA. She'll hear you. She thinks she's fat.

LAYLA. No, not fat. Before was too thin. Now she is a proper woman. She has boyfriend?

ZARA. …Not any more.

LAYLA (*looking around, impressed*). Aliis buy this all by herself?

ZARA. Her parents did.

LAYLA. Oh. That is kind.

ZARA. They're rich, so.

LAYLA. They are nice?

ZARA. Alice always says I'm lucky: She's got money, but my family actually care.

LAYLA. You agree?

ZARA. Mum… I'm sorry about the spotted dick, and dinner, and… everything.

LAYLA. Ya, no problem. English food is horrible. You and Fatima are right to throw on the floor. Next time I make *kleicha*.

ZARA. Is she okay?

LAYLA. She is hurt. Inside. Also her hand.

ZARA *feels terrible. But she's also keen to clear her name.*

ZARA. What she said – about me drinking, / it isn't –

LAYLA. Zahra, when I was fourteen, I had small box under my bed. Inside I had many cassette. American popstars: Michael Jackson, John Travolta. I hide from my mother because I think she would not allow it. But of course, she knows. I always know that you drink.

ZARA. I don't dr– (*Conceding at* LAYLA*'s expression.*) And Dad?

LAYLA. He prefer to believe you don't.

ZARA. Too ashamed of his haram daughter to face the truth?

LAYLA. Your father is not ashamed! He is proud!

ZARA. Dad tells people I'm an immigration lawyer when he knows all I do is answer phones. He boasts about my degree and he must know I nearly failed. At least I was going to marry someone decent. Now not even that. He's ashamed. You all are –

LAYLA. No, Zahra. It is you who are shamed of *us*. (*Before* ZARA *can interrupt.*) We say the wrong thing. We do wrong thing. Tell *truth*, Zahra. We have all lie to each other enough.

ZARA doesn't know how to answer. LAYLA *stands up decisively.*

I will tell truth. When we first come here, we believe we will become so Western, we imagine we will change so much. But then: 'This is not your place!' people is saying. 'Go home, you not wanted!' Your father he feel it very bad. So he try, try to make our life, just like the village, exact same: 'Cook me food like my mother make. Teach my girls what our parents teach us. If this country don't want us, we don't want them.' And every year I feel… is like my life getting smaller. This is hard for our children. To live in two worlds that do not mix. But you should be able to tell your parents, Zahra, if you are unhappy, if you do not want Jamil –

ZARA. Mum –

LAYLA. You should feel you can ask us for help.

She faces ZARA *with authority, this is why she came.*

Come home.

ZARA. What?

LAYLA. Come home to your family.

ZARA. Mum, I can't do that.

LAYLA. Why?

ZARA. Coz I need... I need independence. I know that sounds crazy to you –

LAYLA. Darling, I travel to other side of the world to escape my mother, I understand independence! But sometimes everybody need *help*. Zahra, this morning I call Aliis –

ZARA. Mum! I gave you that number for / emergencies!

LAYLA. She tell me you will not live here any more.

ZARA. I can't just move to Brent.

LAYLA. It will not be Brent.

A beat. ZARA *understands. Remorse overwhelms her.*

ZARA. Oh Mum, I'm / so [sorry]...

LAYLA. Come home. (*Slow, deliberate.*) So we can help you with your illness.

ZARA....What?

At this, LAYLA *fishes in her bag and pulls out some printouts. Pages and pages of paper.*

LAYLA. I print in the internet café. The family does not know.

ZARA. These are colour! How much did you pay?

LAYLA. Twenty pound. Please, Zahra, / read.

ZARA. Right, look. Next time, tell them you only want black and white okay? Or they'll try to rip you / off –

LAYLA. Read, Zahra.

ZARA takes the papers, reads. She freezes. We see they are articles about eating disorders.

ZARA. Why did you bring this?

LAYLA. Last night. Last night for the whole night I read these things. And Zahra, I begin to see so much. I think. I cannot remember last time I see you eat. Eat happy. Food in your mouth. Clean plate. Like when you were young.

ZARA. When I was fat. I eat loads okay? Tons and tons and –

LAYLA. They say this is part of it. The illness.

ZARA. What?

LAYLA. To lie.

ZARA. Google says all kinds of / shit.

LAYLA. Zahra, when you are sick yesterday, was it real? Or you do to yourself?

ZARA. What kind of question is that?

LAYLA. Let me see your eyes.

ZARA. No!

> ZARA *tries to move away but* LAYLA *grabs her face and looks at her eyes.*

LAYLA. Yes, these small red marks. From vomiting. From force.

ZARA. You can't just come in here and…

LAYLA. Zahra, talk to me.

ZARA. There's nothing to talk about!

LAYLA. You are not happy in your life.

ZARA (*almost laughing*). Of course I'm not! Who is?

LAYLA. You have pain. You must tell / me.

ZARA. It's not real pain! It's not running from Saddam, or starving, or giving birth in the back of a van and nearly bleeding to death! I tore you in two, Mum, and you still came back for more! How can I possibly tell you about my stupid – (*Stops herself saying too much.*) Fatima told me you're ill again. And you haven't told Dad. Why are you keeping it secret, Mum?

> LAYLA *looks* ZARA *in the eye but doesn't answer.* ZARA *is caught between pride and frustration.*

You see? *That's* strength. How could you *ever* understand?

LAYLA. Why you say this?

ZARA. Because! You just… shut off your brain and get on with surviving.

LAYLA (*suddenly hard*). I am this simple creature to you?
(*At* ZARA*'s surprise.*) To say this, you make me below you.
You think when people treated me like animal I become
animal, only to eat and sleep and shit and nothing else?

LAYLA *waits for* ZARA *to answer.* ZARA *struggles.*

ZARA. No, I just…

LAYLA. This makes me angry, Zahra. You think there are no
artists, no poets, no great thinkers from our country? That
our stories only are suffering and war? *No*. Everybody,
everybody has a private thoughts inside them, no matter who
they are. And I am sick. I am sick to be called refugee,
immigrant, war victim. Not mother, not woman, not citizen.
Like I never have any dreams. Just *surviving*, like a dog.

…When I was child, your grandfather, sometimes he stop
speaking. Stop eating. Go into the mountains for days and
come back dirty, sick, thin. We wash him, feed him. Never say
anything. To you, he would be a 'simple man'. A shepherd
with an empty brain –

ZARA. Wait, I / didn't –

LAYLA. No dreams but to shit and survive. But inside him,
Zahra, there was a… dark thing. He was a good man. A good
father. He want to take care of us. But the dark thoughts, they
take him away. I use to believe this is his weakness. But when
I come to this country, you are safe, *Alhamdulillah*, thanks to
God, and they can do operation to me, and your baba and me
we having a *home*… I expect that I will be happy. But the
darkness come. Like my father. The darkness come to me and
I cannot leave the bed. You are beside me, you cry. Your baba
begging with me. But for two weeks I do not move.

All children find their own ways. New ways. Parents become
old fashion, stupid to them. I use to feel this with my mother.
I laugh at her, I think she is ignorant. I don't tell her what is
in my mind, I am sure she cannot understand. But, Zahra,
your grandmother have a lot of wisdom. She understand my
baba, better than ever I can. She understand love, and how to
support. And I regret I ignore her now.

…Let me to help you, please.

ZARA. You can't. Trust me. I tried help. And Jamil –

LAYLA. Jamil?

ZARA. Jamil was disgusted. Told me I should be ashamed. After all you've done for me. He didn't want to touch me.

LAYLA. He said this to my daughter?!

ZARA (*matter of fact*). The other night. I was supposed to break up with *him*. I've planned to, so many times. But just like every other time, I thought about you. How disappointed you all would be. So I let him hold my hand, talk about weddings, nod and smile...

And then he started talking about kids. The children we'd have and how we would raise them and my chest... tightened up. Thinking of how my body would change, stop belonging to me, or rip in two like yours did. And what would *I* teach those children? Would they learn to hate me? So I ran. I ran outside, and I... spat it all out. On the pavement. Jamil found me, kneeling in the dirt, vomit down my dress. He *begged* me to let him help. And I thought: 'Okay then. After all, I've known him all my life. I can't spend my life kneeling in the dirt. Maybe I should try telling *someone* the truth...'

When I did, you know what he said?

'You insult your parents. Clean yourself up, woman. No wife of mine is sick on her knees like a dog.' And he walked off. Left me there.

LAYLA (*with quiet fury only a mother can have*). Stupid, stupid boy.

ZARA. He was right. It *is* disgusting.

LAYLA. I never like Jamil.

ZARA. *What?*

LAYLA. I think you love him, so I respect your choice. If I knew this...

Jamil does not speak for me, Zahra. If this is his true colour, it is good he is gone. But *I* am staying. Talk to me. / Talk –

ZARA. I can't. I / can't...

LAYLA. You are *not* disgusting, *talk* –

ZARA. No!

LAYLA. Tell me! (*Grabbing* ZARA*'s hands, almost violent.*)
You are brave! ***Zahra, beautiful, bright, shining, brilliant.***
This is what I name you. *Nothing* can make me to leave you.
Talk!

Struck by her mother's passion, ZARA *finally releases. It
comes out in a jumble. Painful, messy, like vomit.*

ZARA. It's a hole, like this black hole, in front of me, I dream
it, I see it, wherever I go it's there... it's going to swallow
me up... I'm bad, ugly, dirty and the hole is coming for me.
What can I hold on to? To stop me falling in? My body. My
body, yeah. Bad, ugly, dirty, but at least I can... hold it. Pull
at it. Control. Nothing crosses these lips. Hunger pangs and
cries in the night, but I rule you, nothing can cross these lips.
I run my hands over the new ribs that emerge, but the hole...
the hole is still there. And I get good. I get clever... I hide
my enemy in tissues, spit it out, my secret, nothing can cross
these lips. If it does I fail. If I fail then, black bile, retching,
throat on fire, heaving, sick and sick and sick, eyes
streaming, gasping for breath, but nothing can cross these
lips. If it does then I fall in. Coz what else is there to believe
in? What other rules can I live by?

ZARA stops, spent. A silence. LAYLA *moves towards*
ZARA. *At first* ZARA *is wary. But as* LAYLA *draws near
and opens her arms,* ZARA *succumbs. She falls into her
mother, as if years have fallen away and* ZARA *is a tiny child
again. They hold each other.* LAYLA *strokes* ZARA*'s hair.*

(*Small.*) I'm sorry. After everything you taught me, about
hunger and –

LAYLA. No more sorry. You are sick, but you will fight it. You
have the blood of fighters.

ZARA. But I'm not you, Mama, I'm not them. I'm weak...

LAYLA. You are not weak. You are many things, but not weak.
You are all the people that come before you. All the ones you

meet, you are the decisions you making. You choose who to be, Zahra, you do not have to choose just one thing. You will fight.

ZARA. How do you know?

LAYLA. Because you are my daughter.

Beat. ZARA *looks up at her mother.*

ZARA. Mama?

LAYLA. *Aiwa.*

ZARA. How did you get out of bed?

LAYLA *contemplates this.*

LAYLA. I have to work very hard. I have to say: Layla, you are ill. But is not your fault. I put the bad thoughts outside my body. It is not easy. Sometimes still I see them, sitting in the corner of the room. But I think, Layla, stay alive. For your daughters. Your family. You *all* save me, Zahra. And your father, also he help so much. Very patient. Listening. Never criticise me.

ZARA. Dad?

LAYLA. There are many things you do not know about your father, Zahra.

ZARA *considers this. She stops* LAYLA *stroking her hair and faces her.*

ZARA. Mama. How sick are you?

LAYLA. The bad things from before. It comes back. I must have… hysterectomy.

ZARA. What? When did you find out?!

LAYLA. A few month.

ZARA. You've not told Baba? You've been going to the hospital? Alone?

LAYLA. Yes.

ZARA. Oh, Mama, I'm so sorry.

LAYLA. Why you are sorry?

ZARA. I should have been there, translating! Like I always did. You should've told me, let me help.

LAYLA. You wish this? To help me?

ZARA. Of course.

LAYLA. Okay. If you let me to help *you*. (*Before* ZARA *can protest*.) It is sickness, Zahra. It must heal or it will kill you. You know this. Come *home* and we will take care of each other. This is my deal. Take or leave.

ZARA doesn't know how to answer. She steps away to bring her mother the tea. LAYLA *accepts it, takes a sip.* ZARA *studies her.*

ZARA. Is it okay?

LAYLA (*hiding her disgust*). Is... very nice.

ZARA. You hate it.

LAYLA. No, no is delicious. I will... drink later.

ZARA (*takes a sip, puts it down*). You're right, it's gross.

LAYLA. This is how English drink tea?

ZARA. It's how hipsters drink it.

LAYLA. Hipster...

Beat. LAYLA *stands, making a decision.*

Yallah! I cannot drink this tea, and I am hungry from the long, *long* journey to your house. You take me to this café outside and we will order 'hipster breakfast'. (*At* ZARA*'s hesitance, gentle.*) If you cannot eat, is okay. We take small step.

ZARA. That... would be nice.

LAYLA. Good. But none of this, like Fatima say... pull-porky!

ZARA (*laughing*). Obviously!

Beat. LAYLA *proceeds, gentle, but with authority.*

LAYLA. And then… we will come here. We will pack your bags. We will go home. And we will tell your baba and your sister. Both of us, together. We will get well again. Step by step.

ZARA is silent. On the other side of the space, FATIMA enters.

Zahra?

ZARA.… You don't have to do this.

LAYLA. I want to. To know each other better. There is time.

They exit, as FATIMA takes centre-stage.

Epilogue

Fatima's Song

FATIMA *plays her music out loud. Taking advantage of having the house to herself, she performs her song as a whole for the first time.*

'Out of Sorts'

Verse

You ask me where I'm from
So where do I start?
Ask my parents where they're from
What's home at heart?

Ask my fearless mother
Fleeing death and dark
Ask my baba beaten blue
Still got strength to laugh?

Chorus

England's not our home
England's not our space
But we have hopes for you
It will be your place, yeah it will be your place

Verse

Ask my sister – see her smile
How she chose a mask
Be let in, shed her skin
Her truth, her past?

Ask this place that treats us
Like who we are is wrong
The only place I know
And still I don't belong

England's not our home, England's not our… nah.

FATIMA *stops. The words aren't right. She listens to the music, searching for something. Suddenly she stops the track, straightens up.* FATIMA *faces forward, singing with confidence and passion.*

Chorus

If England ain't our home,
Then I stand here caught
So I claim the right
To be outta –

FATIMA *hears the key in the lock and immediately stops singing.* LAYLA *enters, followed by* ZARA, *pulling a suitcase. The women look at each other.* FATIMA *takes the suitcase.*

Blackout.

A Nick Hern Book

Out of Sorts first published in Great Britain in 2019 as a paperback original by Nick Hern Books Limited, The Glasshouse, 49a Goldhawk Road, London W12 8QP, in association with Theatre503

Out of Sorts copyright © 2019 Danusia Samal

Danusia Samal has asserted her moral right to be identified as the author of this work

Cover artwork by Rebecca Pitt

Designed and typeset by Nick Hern Books, London
Printed in the UK by Mimeo Ltd, Huntingdon, Cambridgeshire PE29 6XX

A CIP catalogue record for this book is available from the British Library

ISBN 978 1 84842 899 7

Woodland
CARBON
www.woodlandcarbon.co.uk
NICK HERN BOOKS
Printed on Carbon Captured paper

www.nickhernbooks.co.uk

facebook.com/nickhernbooks

twitter.com/nickhernbooks